Trippett

ASPERGER'S ON THE JOB

MUST-HAVE ADVICE
FOR PEOPLE WITH
ASPERGER'S or
High Functioning Autism
and their Employers,
Educators, and Advocates

RUDY SIMONE

FUTURE HORIZONS INC.
ARLINGTON, TEXAS

ASPERGER'S ON THE JOB

All marketing and publishing rights guaranteed to and reserved by:

FUTURE HORIZONS INC.

721 W. Abram Street
Arlington, Texas 76013
800-489-0727
817-277-0727
817-277-2270 (fax)
E-mail: *info@FHautism.com*
www.FHautism.com

Book design © TLC Graphics, www.TLCGraphics.com
Cover by: Monica Thomas; Interior by: Erin Stark

Cover photo courtesy of: www.istock.com

Printed in the United States of America.

Publisher's Cataloging-In-Publication Data
(Prepared by The Donohue Group, Inc.)

Simone, Rudy.
    Aspergers on the job : must-have advice for people with Asperger's or high functioning autism and their employers, educators, and advocates / Rudy Simone.

    p. ; cm.

    Includes bibliographical references and index.
    ISBN: 978-1-935274-09-4

1. Asperger's syndrome--Patients--Employment. 2. Asperger's syndrome--Patients--Vocational guidance. 3. Developmentally disabled--Employment. 4. Developmentally disabled--Vocational guidance. I. Title.

HD7255 .S56 2010

331.59/5

To my daughter Lena,
who patiently watched while I figured it out.

Table
of Contents

Foreword

by Temple Grandin, Ph.D.

Having a career enables me to have an interesting life—one where I can use my mind to do work that others value and appreciate. People on the autism spectrum can do a variety of jobs ranging from high level technical or creative careers to entry-level jobs. Since I was socially awkward, I convinced large corporations to hire me for designing livestock equipment by showing a portfolio of drawings and photos of completed projects. Many people thought I was weird, but when they saw my drawings, they said, "Wow, you drew that?" Then they hired me.

I chose the freelance career route and worked as a freelance designer for the first twenty years of my career. The freelance route helped me avoid a lot of social problems. I went to the client's workplace, designed the project, and was gone in a few days or weeks. I did all my drawing and design work in a quiet office at home. Later, when I was in my early forties, I got a part-time position as a professor at Colorado State University. I remain employed there and I have still been able to continue my freelance work.

I have been very fortunate to find a career I can thrive in, but it didn't happen by chance. Many teachers and mentors supported me and helped me find success. Similarly, I believe this book will help people on the spectrum find enriching careers that suit their individual needs and talents. It will also help teachers and family members to assist people on the spectrum as they enter the workforce. There is a lot in this book that I wish I'd known when I was young. The following is advice for people with Asperger's based on my personal experience, to add to and complement Ms. Simone's insightful ideas and strategies.

1. Use your area of strength.

In my work, I used my visual thinking, which was my area of strength. As a visual thinker, I can test-run equipment in my head like a three-dimensional, virtual-reality computer. Another individual may have a different area of strength. From discussions with hundreds of individuals on the spectrum, I have learned that the areas of strength tend to fall into three basic types. They are: 1) visual thinkers, 2) pattern thinkers (music and math minds), and 3) word-detail thinkers. Visual thinkers are well suited for jobs such as graphic design, computer animation, architecture, working with animals, and industrial design. The pattern thinkers are often good at computer programming, mathematics, and statistics. The word-detail thinkers may excel at technical writing, journalism, record-keeping jobs, and specialized sales jobs. I know several individuals with Asperger's who work in retail and are appreciated for their extensive knowledge of the merchandise. One may ask, how can an Aspie handle a sales job if he or she has social challenges? Well, business interactions can be very different from other social interactions; they are often scripted, like a play. For example, I was really good at selling advertising for a cattle magazine, after I got over my initial fears. I have even "worked" on a retail sales floor. I was doing a book signing at a Costco® store when a rare opportunity arose. Since no one was coming up to the book table, I started walking the sales floor and selling books. I walked up to couples and families and asked them about their pets. I just repeated a short script and wound up selling 65 hardcover books in six hours. I had never

worked a retail floor before, but I found that I was quite good at it. So never underestimate what you can do.

2. Request accommodations.

I chose not to disclose to clients that I had autism, but I did request certain accommodations that made it easier (or in some cases, possible) to do my job. To avoid errors and miscommunication, I always asked for very explicit instructions to clarify what people expected of me. Sometimes, that was tricky. I didn't want to ask for so many details that my clients felt they were designing the project themselves, but I had to know the specifics regarding what the proposed piece of equipment was supposed to *do*. For example, one client needed equipment that could handle 200 cattle per hour, but they had only three people available at a time to run it. The client's instructions did not clarify that; it only said the equipment had to be "labor efficient." That was too vague! So be sure to ask your supervisors and/or clients to tell you exactly what they want. I also had problems remembering long strings of verbal instructions. I had to take notes at project meetings so I had a record of what the specifications for a project were. If you have similar issues, or even if you don't, it is a good idea to get clear instructions in writing so you have something concrete to refer to over the course of your project. This can help you avoid dissatisfied supervisors and clients.

Sometimes, the biggest obstacle for an employee with Asperger's who is working in an office, factory, or retail store is his or her sensory sensitivities. Some individuals on the spectrum cannot tolerate the flicker of fluorescent light bulbs; to them, it can feel like they are in a disco with strobe lights. Others cannot tolerate a lot of background noise while they work. This book has lots of helpful advice on sensory accommodations. I really related to the discussion about open offices. It would have been impossible for me to draw my designs if I had to sit in a noisy office. Like most people on the spectrum, I need a quiet place in order to do my best work. Sensory sensitivities can vary extremely, so it is important to find, or create, a sensory environment that is conducive to *your* needs.

3. Avoid jealousy.

One of the worst problems I had to deal with was my coworkers' jealousy. At one workplace, I was hired by the general manager to design a project and supervise its installation. The resident engineer felt that I had invaded his turf, so he "bad-mouthed" my work to the other managers. In a different workplace, my equipment was deliberately damaged by other employees. I even heard about one sad case where a jealous coworker planted pornographic material on an Aspie's computer in an attempt to get him fired. The jealous coworker felt insecure about his own talent and was worried that the Aspie's drawings were "too good."

I learned to combat jealousy by allowing the jealous person to be more involved in my project. I would ask the person for advice or compliment him/her on the equipment that he/she had built. I learned that people got jealous because designing was so easy for me. I usually finished a drawing really quickly, but to avoid jealousy, I would often wait two for three days before I would send it to the client. Sometimes, even if you've done nothing wrong, it is smart to take these kinds of steps to avoid problems that could jeopardize the success of your project.

4. Prevent potential employment problems.

During my travels, I have observed two problems that can ruin a job for a person with Asperger's, even if he/she has been successful in that position for many years. The first, ironically, is promotion. I have talked to several individuals on the spectrum who used to have good jobs in areas such as drafting/design, sports writing, and research science, but they lost their jobs after being promoted into management. They just could not handle the stress. For some people, it would be best to avoid the promotion.

Another source of conflict is a change in existing management. If a sympathetic supervisor is replaced by a less supportive one, that can ruin the career of an employee who is on the spectrum. Certain differences may no longer be tolerated, and the work environment can quickly evolve into a very unpleasant one until the employee leaves or is fired.

If this or some other unfortunate situation does occur and the person loses his/her job, other issues often come to light, such as the employee's failure to preserve copies of their work. I talked to several older Aspies who lost their jobs when their company was reorganized and they had never saved any examples of their work for their portfolios. All of their work was left behind. One person was an engineer who had failed to preserve samples of his drawings. Another person failed to save samples of the sales manual he had written. I learned that, to be successful, I had to show samples of my work to potential employers instead of selling myself. A good portfolio, in addition to a resume, can help you get many types of jobs. You need to save and take home paper copies of your best work (electronic media are useless when they become obsolete). To avoid problems with confidentiality, you can show only small portions of your drawings or written documents. Your portfolio should be professionally presented and should include four or five examples of your best work. Choose examples that would be appropriate for the job you are seeking. For example, if you were applying for a journalism job, articles you had written for a high school newspaper should be in your portfolio. However, articles on extreme politics, sex, or religion should never be included. Your work life will be more successful if you leave these subjects at home. It is a good idea to build a strong professional portfolio, even if you expect to stay in your current position for a long time. Sometimes things happen that are out of your control, and you need to be prepared.

If you found this advice helpful, you are really going to love this book. It is especially helpful to individuals on the high end of the autism spectrum who will be working full-time in the same workplace every day. The sections on dealing with social problems at the office are especially valuable.

During my career, I have worked for twenty major clients and over two hundred smaller ones. If I had read this book when I was in my twenties, I could have avoided many problems with coworkers.

I truly believe that this book will help individuals on the autism spectrum get, and keep, the fulfilling jobs that they deserve. And the whole world will benefit from their passion and ingenuity.

TEMPLE GRANDIN, PH.D.

Author of *Thinking in Pictures, Developing Talents,*
and *The Way I See It*

Introduction

While I was researching my book *22 Things a Woman Must Know If She Loves a Man With Asperger's Syndrome* (2009) I discovered a strong recurring theme: the majority of adults with Asperger's I spoke to had great difficulty earning a living. Most were on unemployment, welfare, or disability; some were still living off their parents; others were surviving only because they were married and their spouse had a good income and health insurance. Many were self-employed, some successfully, but most in that category were jacks-of-all-trades scraping out a living through a variety of odd jobs. Their experiences echoed my own—I had thought I was the only one who, despite many practical gifts, did not fit into the world of full-time employment. This has colored every aspect of my life and has negatively impacted my self-esteem, finances, relationships, and health. Finding out that so many others were going through these same struggles, I felt compelled to do something about it. I began to research and list all the factors involved in determining whether or not an employment experience is successful for both parties—employer and AS employee.

I've come to the conclusion that there are cultural differences between those with the syndrome and those without. Those differences are felt most keenly in the workplace, where a person is essentially held captive for a large portion of their day. Think about the differences in communication, different physical needs, different needs in instructions and supervision, different outlooks on time constraints; when you add into the mix the AS person's social anxieties and independent spirit, there is a lot of potential for failure. Yet, those with Asperger's possess some extremely useful, important, creative, and marketable skills that employers are missing out on. Likewise, employers hold the paychecks, and those are what people with AS are largely missing out on. With the autistic population on the rise the way that it is, there's going to have to be some kind of compromise. Times are tough, and while the economy of people with Asperger's has always been bad, it's just going to get worse in a competitive job market. It is thought that over 85% of people with AS are without fulltime employment. This situation is bound to have dire consequences on the health and security of the individuals affected, as well as on their families and their communities.

This book is a resource to help employers accommodate this growing population, and for this growing population to find and keep gainful employment. The only way that we can do that is to know what our strengths are and use them productively. A lot of us with Asperger's don't always realize what our strengths are because we have been told throughout our lives that these characteristics are flaws—or else we receive mixed messages. For example, we are told to work hard and when we do, we fail because of our social skills. We also need to know where we are sabotaging our own best interests.

Employers and corporations have been going down a certain path for a long time now. With cost-saving techniques being implemented, whether in the form of lay-offs, cramped open-plan offices, energy-efficient fluorescent lights in windowless rooms, or no fully-subsidized health care plan, things are becoming less secure, less pleasant for all. The rise of stringent hiring procedures and screening in the form of personality tests has

given rise to an atmosphere of conformity and play-it-safe behaviors, leaving many feeling restricted and unfulfilled. This is difficult enough for non-spectrum people, but even worse for those with AS who are socially and environmentally sensitive, and who have a hard time coloring inside the lines or thinking inside the box.

This book looks into all aspects of employment—because going to work isn't just about work. It's about what you wear, what you eat, what your environment looks like, what it feels like, how your boss behaves, and how your coworkers treat you. There's so much more to a job than what the tasks are. Most people with Asperger's would just like to do the work and go home, but life's not that simple. I wish I could say I have the magic formula to ensuring a harmonious experience for all, but people are people and is it very difficult to mandate human behavior except in its most obvious and extreme forms. Many of the difficulties we will discuss are subtle in nature—subtle, but insidious at times, and with real and often serious consequences. It is very important to recognize our differences and to become aware of some of the injustices this population has experienced, from ostracism to verbal abuse to physical assault on the job, often with management turning a blind eye to these events because of inherent prejudice towards those who are different.

Asperger's Syndrome: An Autism Spectrum Disorder

Autism is not a disease; it is a neurological disorder which is now largely considered to be the result of genetic and environmental factors. While there is much debate over autism's exact cause, one thing is certain: there is no doubt that the number of people affected by autism has risen dramatically. The Centers for Disease Control has just confirmed that prevalence is now 1 in 100 (CDC 2009). Less than twenty years ago, prevalence was at 1 in 10,000! Only some of this increase is due to changes in when and how autism is diagnosed. These numbers include everyone on the *autism spectrum*, from the more severe and obvious classic or low-functioning autism, on to High-Functioning Autism (HFA), and to the mildest form, known as Asperger's Syndrome (AS).

Depending upon whom you ask, there appears to be little difference between HFA and Asperger's. Most say it is a question of IQ, yet I've met those who were diagnosed HFA and were highly intelligent. Diagnosing autism is itself not an exact science; it is identified mostly by its symptoms and there is always some level of subjectivity involved. At the time of this writing, there is debate over whether to abolish the Asperger's diagnosis altogether, and merely place it back under the heading of autism. Whether or not that happens, the condition, the subculture, and the challenges of those at the high functioning end of the autism spectrum will remain unique, and must continue to be the subject of study and redress. Another point to bear in mind is that as young autistic children improve over time, through the efforts of family, diets, doctors, and support teams, they may no longer be classed as autistic, but will likely share at least some of the traits of Asperger's. For the sake of simplicity, we will use the term Asperger's (AS) to mean anyone at the higher end of the spectrum.

The reader will notice that throughout this book, I sometime use "we" when referring to Aspergians and other times "they." I felt it was not only important to illustrate that I know firsthand what I'm writing of, but also that my experiences are not exactly the same as another's, and that it would be erroneous and simplistic to promote the idea that we all have the same strengths and weaknesses, the same experiences. There are themes, threads, and similarities, but I don't ever wish to convey a one-size-fits-all picture or make the reader feel as if I am speaking clinically. I sometimes find it offensive when even the most well-meaning individual refers to us as "they," but unfortunately that cannot be helped, and I wish to keep the focus off myself and on others.

You can find the criteria for Asperger's, from the Diagnostic and Statistical Manual of Mental Disorders, 4th Edition (DSM-IV), easily enough online. But it's not really going to bring it to life for you in human terms. Generally, people with Asperger's are highly intelligent. They frequently have savant skills or abilities in one or more areas. They are generally uncomfortable around other people because of a fight-or-flight reaction to social contact that can make them seem anti-social, unfriendly, or intimidated. They often

have difficulty communicating verbally, and are socially awkward. They sometimes talk to themselves or echo what has been said to them. They may suffer bouts of mutism and shyness. Conversely, if they are talking about a subject they are interested in, they can speak at great length, and, because they have difficulty understanding social cues, may go on when no one is really interested. There are physical hallmarks of AS, such as low muscle tone or poor posture, and trouble with eye contact. The reasons for all these things will be discussed in this book. While Asperger's is often called the "geek syndrome," that's not always the way a person with AS appears; they may appear quite cool at times, attractive, artistic; or they may just seem quirky or eccentric. It presents differently among individuals and also between genders.

Dr. Barbara Nichols, founder of the Southern Arizona Association of Adult Asperger's, further describes it for us in easy-to-understand terms:

> Aspergians usually want to be social but find it nearly impossible to figure out how to behave in a social setting or how to maintain social relationships. They have trouble reading and understanding body language, facial expressions, voice tones, or idioms. It is as if they were from an alien culture and were never taught the meaning of subtle gestures and nuances of conversation. They can't figure out the rules of engagement in a social exchange. It is awkward for them to jump into a conversation and they report that they can't figure out how to add to the discussion without taking it off the track. Add to the above list of characteristics a long list of symptoms such as anxiety, depression, obsessive compulsive disorder, attention deficit hyperactivity disorder, tic disorders, and learning disabilities, and you are getting closer to what it is to be an Aspergian. They struggle with sleep, eating, digestive, and sensory problems, all of which make melding into the social environment difficult. In addition, many, if not most, Aspergians had been bullied in school and have trauma-related disorders as a result. Most often,

they are rejected, or worse, made fun of in the workplace and in school. Loneliness is their constant companion.

Asperger's has its advantages. [People with this disorder] can hyperfocus on one topic and have a tenacity that is matchless. They can store huge amounts of information, learn languages easily, and are talented scientists, musicians, technicians, and historians. While they are not comfortable with people, they love information. Aspergians are in good company. Albert Einstein, Alexander Graham Bell, Thomas Edison, and Sir Isaac Newton, just to name a few, are now thought to have had Asperger's Syndrome. More recently, actor Dan Aykroyd has announced that he has been diagnosed with Asperger's Syndrome. Once they have learned that they are not inferior, but rather exquisitely different, they begin to appreciate themselves and their considerable talents. The culture at large has not accepted them as yet. Finding a niche in the world is what is needed and those lucky enough to find it excel and contribute significantly. (2009)

Despite these positive traits, people with AS often have difficulty obtaining and keeping jobs. The main reasons boil down to:

- Awkward social skills
- Difficulty communicating
- Environmental sensitivity
- Not being able to utilize their natural strengths and inherent interests

In the workplace "their failure to adhere to social rules often results in ridicule, aggression, or exclusion" (Hendrickx 2009) until they are literally driven out—either fired or ostracized until life at work becomes unbearable and they quit. Consequently, many with AS have a patchwork quilt for a resume: an inordinate number of jobs, gaps between jobs, or a long history of self-employment in one or even several fields. Yet, this kind of track record can be a boon for both employer and AS employee, for a varied history usually makes for a wide variety of useful skills. It is important that a

potential employer does not assume that this history stems from a lack of desire to work. There may not be a harder-working segment of the human race. The AS person simply may not have had:

a. the diagnosis and understanding of AS to know what they needed from an employer, or

b. an employer who was willing to listen and to make the easy but crucial adjustments to accommodate them.

This book will help the person with AS understand and ask for what they need, and it will show the employer how easy it is to give them what they need—which often involves doing *less* rather than more.

Over a seven-month period, more than fifty adults with Asperger's were interviewed for this book hailing from all over America, and other countries such as Japan, Ireland, England, France, and Australia. They were asked to describe their work experiences in their own words: their successes, their failures, and what they felt they needed to succeed in employment. They all had very similar experiences and wishes, regardless of whether they barely made it through high school or had postgraduate degrees, and no matter what color their collar was. In addition to this anecdotal information, many others were contacted: psychologists, autism cause-and-cure researchers, government disability benefit agencies, university disability offices, as well as founders of Asperger's education/work-study programs. They provided information on the latest research, statistics, laws, rights, programs, and other such information pertaining to all aspects of Asperger's Syndrome, most notably, employment. I would like to thank all of them for their participation. I would also like to give a special nod of thanks to Dr. Nichols, who graciously shared her expertise; to Roger N. Meyer, who gave me much-needed encouragement during the final stretch; and to Dr. Temple Grandin, whose heart and wit are as great as her intellect.

1

Why Should You Employ Someone with AS?

The Advantages of Asperger's Syndrome in the Workplace

he question everyone asks is "why would an employer hire someone for whom he/she has to make special accommodation?"

First, the ASD population is growing in numbers. So much so, that avoiding hiring someone with AS is nearly infeasible for larger businesses or certain fields. Some experts believe that, due to these rising numbers, it is now necessary to provide employers with autism awareness training, similar to how sexual harassment training is required.

Second, people with AS by and large have to work, and to find and maintain employment without significant support. Financial benefits are very hard to obtain, at least in the U.S., because in most states one would have to be *mentally retarded* to be eligible for state or federally-funded

assistance programs designed for people with *developmental* disabilities. Also, there are still very few vocational support services for people with Asperger's and other ASDs.

Third and most importantly, the gifts and abilities that many with AS possess far outweigh the relatively minor inconvenience of making adjustments, which have more to do with mindset than anything else.

What are these gifts, how do we use them, and how can they sometimes work against us?

1. **Focus and diligence.** The Aspergian ability to focus on tasks for a long period of time without needing supervision or incentive is legendary. We are hard workers. The downside of this trait is that we can be focusing on the wrong things or getting so involved in what we enjoy doing that other things fall by the wayside. If our passion is not our vocation, we who have Asperger's may neglect actually making money.

2. **We take pride in our work,** no matter how small the task. This ensures a job done with conscience. But again, if money is not a big motivating factor, then a person may do work because they like it, rather than for decent pay or a living wage. And at some point, if the work isn't meaningful, enthusiasm will wane.

3. **A desire to please.** While it may not always seem so, we often really do desire to fit in. We will extend ourselves to do a good job, to get approval.

4. **Independent, unique thinking.** People with AS march to their own drum. We tend to spend a lot of time alone and develop our own unique thoughts as opposed to having a "herd" mentality. While a team-player attitude can be a plus in the workplace, a person who has the courage to walk their own line will more likely come up with novel and creative ideas.

5. Higher fluid intelligence. Scientists in Japan have recently discovered that AS children have a higher *fluid intelligence* than non-autistic children (Hayashi, Kato, Igarashi, Kashima 2008). Fluid intelligence is "the ability to find meaning in confusion and solve new problems; the ability to draw inferences and understand the relationships of various concepts, independent of acquired knowledge" (Wikipedia 2009). We do not however, have a higher *crystallized* intelligence—which is the ability to apply acquired knowledge and skills. Think of us as strongly intuitive, intelligent in a sixth-sense kind of way, in some cases genius, but perhaps lacking in certain areas of common sense.

> **"The boss referred to me as 'the corporation's mad genius' and then said he meant it 'in a good way.'"**
>
> **– LEWIS, BA HISTORY, 51, UNEMPLOYED**

6. Visual, three-dimensional thinking. Some people with AS are very visual in their thought processes, which lends itself to countless useful and creative applications in the work environment. Temple Grandin, author of *Thinking in Pictures* (1995, 2006), is perhaps the most famous visual thinker on the spectrum. She is able to visualize large-scale projects, draw up blueprints, and then accurately test-run them in her mind before they are built.

7. Attention to detail, sometimes with painstaking perfection, again ensuring a job well done. One flipside of this can be wanting to spend more time on a task than an employer or coworkers might wish.

> **"I got far too involved with talking about and notating every detail of the conversation with my customer. I had very long calls but did the best job for that reason."**
>
> **– MIA, 40, UNEMPLOYED**

8. Honesty. The value of being able to say "the emperor isn't wearing any clothes" should not be underestimated, even if it's not what people want to hear. This can make a person unpopular. Sometimes it manifests as brutal honesty, and lacking in tact or thought of consequences.

9. Logic over emotion. Although people with AS can be very sensitive, we spend so much time "computing" in our minds that we get quite good at it. We can be very logical in our approach to problem-solving. Of course there are times, even in business, that a more empathic, emotion-driven response is called for.

What are your or your employee's positive qualities?
Are you currently using them to your advantage?

The Importance of Belief

The general public has little idea what autism really is, and even less about Asperger's. They don't know how it presents, or what it looks like. People are shocked when they see an attractive or intelligent person who announces they are on the spectrum—as if we are always talking to ourselves or twirling in circles. While some with AS are more obviously affected, it is harder to spot in others. For brief periods of time, many with Asperger's Syndrome can appear completely non-autistic and "normal." But many (myself included) say that it exhausts them to do so and they can't keep it up for long. If a person is "on" at a particular day or time, no one might ever guess that they were autistic. And even when we do act "different," autism is not the label that springs to mind. Awkward, rude, nervous, shy, strange, slow, arrogant: these are the types of labels that often get pinned on us.

While at times there may be some apparent anomalies in our manner, expression, or gait, the general rule is that you can't tell by just looking whether or not someone has Asperger's. Hence, it is often called the "invisible syndrome." Idiosyncratic behavior is occasional, and it is usually triggered by social or environmental things.

If you are an employer, you may have hired someone who impressed you with their skills, their resume, and their qualities, and then, as time passes, they cause you to wonder. They may seem to lack common sense or people skills. They might be the most efficient or hardworking person on your staff but also, perhaps, the most abrasive at times. They may withdraw from coworkers and acquire a "reputation" as a result. The more you try to talk to them about or question their behavior, the more withdrawn, even sullen, they might get. You then become suspicious or confused, and wonder if you were fooled or lied to at their interview. You may think that they don't like the job. Often that is not the case; social and environmental factors will be the cause of this behavior and, as you read on, you will come to know exactly what those factors are.

People with Asperger's seem to fall into one of two camps regarding interviews and first impressions. They either interview very poorly, and have difficulty getting jobs they qualify for because of it, or else they interview really well and have little difficulty obtaining jobs. That is because the interview is a short performance; it is keeping the job that will be difficult. You may be dazzled at the interview by this employee, and then wonder at the difference in them as the days and weeks go by. Most people with AS will agree with the statement "familiarity breeds contempt," for as time passes, their AS behaviors will have begun to be witnessed, provoking a reaction from coworkers that can range from bemused, to condescending, to hostile. A person with AS who carries him- or herself professionally, gracefully and who has achieved things academically and in their career, has had to struggle to do so. The very fact that they appear "normal" is a good thing, an achievement, but should not be an indication that they do not have Asperger's or that they do not struggle. Some of the leaders in the field of AS research and education are highly intelligent, eloquent people who have AS, or were even

diagnosed with classic autism as children. Through a myriad of methods such as observation, support from family, friends, therapists, organizations, reading; research; etc., they have come to the place of "normalcy" that they now occupy. But it has not been easy for them and most likely remains a situation of constant focus, effort, and vigilance.

> "In most people's minds, a disability is something you can see plainly, something tangible. Asperger's, sadly, doesn't fall into that category, and beyond knowing of it, most employers have very little understanding of what it entails, with a degree of ignorance similar to that shown to dyslexics years ago."
>
> – SEAN, 29, UK, FILM STUDENT

One situation many with AS encounter is that they are often told they don't seem autistic, or that their struggles are no different than anyone else's. AJ Mahari, an Asperger's Syndrome educator who lives in Canada, says this on the subject:

> One thing I hear sometimes from people is, "You don't seem like you have Asperger's" or "it doesn't seem like you have it that bad." Maybe that's good; but sometimes it feels invalidating, a little less than respectful of my life experience and what I struggle with. ...Really what's behind that is a tremendous legacy of work. If you only knew what I have had to map out, read about, learn, study, analyze, process, slice and dice, and put back together in my own way; I mean, virtually everything. I've had to do a lot of work to be able to do what I do. (2009)

Asperger's was not recognized by the American Psychiatric Association (entered into the DSM-IV) until 1994. Prior to that, people with AS were either undiagnosed, or worse, misdiagnosed and put on medications such as Ritalin for conditions they did not have. They will not have had the understanding, support, and training that youngsters with AS are now beginning to receive. AS adults have had to come up through life and learn

by their own tenacity, ingenuity, and mettle. This in itself will show you what strength, intelligence, adaptability, and problem-solving skills most of us possess. Currently, all over the world, adults of all ages are receiving their first correct diagnosis, and breathing a sigh of relief as they realize they are *not* difficult, crazy, or alone ... that there *is* a name for what they have.

A word on diagnosis: If a person has not been diagnosed by a doctor (i.e., they are self-diagnosed), don't assume it is for lack of trying:

- In the U.S., diagnoses can be *very* expensive ($800-$2000) and are often not covered by insurance.

- Nearly half the Americans interviewed for this book had no health insurance anyway.

- It is important that a diagnosis be given by someone who has, as Dr. Barbara Nichols put it, "comprehensive knowledge of the syndrome, and an appreciation for the syndrome as a whole picture, versus a collection of symptoms." These professionals are still relatively few in number.

- Diagnosis is particularly problematic for adults. By the time a person has reached maturity the outward signs of AS have usually become less visible. And since part of diagnosis involves the doctor interviewing relatives of the AS person, if family members don't recall or are in denial about what went on several decades ago, that could be counterproductive.

It is important that employers, advocates, family, etc., do not doubt the diagnosis. While I'm sure there are those who get their self-diagnosis wrong, if they have most of the traits of AS then the same methods of coping, the same strategies will apply. In addition, it is important that you do not doubt the *capabilities* of the person with Asperger's. Being misread, doubted, having our positive qualities overlooked, and being blamed for our "faults," is quite common among us.

What the employee can do:

- Take such comments as "you don't seem like you are autistic" as a compliment rather than becoming defensive or feeling negated. What they are saying is that you seem capable, social, and intelligent. If you choose to keep your autism secret from some people, then this is exactly what you wanted. If you generally disclose, then you are doing your part to educate the world about Asperger's Syndrome.

- Do not give up on a proper diagnosis if you don't have one yet. Persist with the powers that be until you do, as it may afford you legal protection and other advantages down the line.

- Don't blame yourself for being autistic and don't internalize the guilt others lay on you for being different. Just learn to manage less positive behaviors.

To employers and advocates:

- While the possibility is there that a person may be misdiagnosed, or inaccurately self-diagnosed, it has been my experience in researching this book that most who claim to have AS have done their research and feel quite confident that the syndrome fits their profile. AS is not something that someone would *want* to have, just to get special attention or concessions. It is something that so strongly defines who you are that you must acknowledge it to explain why you do the things you do. Too often we get accused by friends, family, loved ones, and those who are supposed to help us, of using Asperger's as a "crutch." It is not an excuse, it is a reason.

- If your employee blew you away at interview only to have a swift and steep decline, don't think they lied to you or misrepresented themselves and their abilities. Understand that the capable, confident person that you hired is in there, but is getting diminished or obscured by certain environmental or social aspects of the job. The rest of this book will describe exactly what those factors are and how to deal with them.

Describe what Asperger's means to you—
what it is and how you feel about it.

Are your thoughts about it primarily negative
or do you see the gifts?

The Big Consequences of Small Talk

ne of the first things that coworkers will notice, long before bosses do, is that people with AS are no good at small talk. While researching this book, the one thing that virtually all respondents had in common was that they didn't know how to socialize on the job. Some had tried and failed to master the art of chitchat and subsequently came to despise it. Many felt they should not *have* to socialize on the job, that it was superfluous and unnecessary to the performance of their duties.

There are a few reasons why small talk may be difficult for some with Asperger's. First, we are practical and tend to have narrow interests. Why talk about something that isn't, in one's own opinion, worth talking about? Second, while non-autistic people see social interaction as meaning safety and security, folks with AS perceive social interaction as being dangerous; people stimulate our amygdala (the *fight-or-flight* reaction). Given that information, it is quite easy to

see how being relaxed around others enough to engage in chitchat might be a challenge. So although rocket science may be easy for a person with Asperger's, small talk and socializing often are impenetrable mysteries:

> **"Small talk is deadly for me. I am expected to talk with them about babies, boyfriends, shopping, and gossip. I try but then I become exhausted and resentful and can't keep up."**
>
> **– ALLISON, 39, BA**

A person with Asperger's will go to work—to work. They are NOT there to win a popularity contest. Unfortunately, they find that reality is different—that they are expected not just to perform the job, but also to succeed socially. Most said that they need an understanding of the "unspoken job requirements" or "hidden agenda," and that their job failures had been due to their inability to socialize, rather than anything to do with actual job performance. Although some learn how to socialize over time, none seem to know how to do it inherently. An Aspergian may be able to talk for hours on their favorite subject, but bring up a local sports team or the weather, and they're stumped (unless that is one of their obsessions).

If a person with AS is in an environment with like-minded people (esp. with shared interests), then this will not be an issue for them. This is sometimes the case with younger people who are still in college or those who work in a more tolerant, cerebral, or specialized atmosphere. However, should their job ever end, or when they finish college and they try to work in different environments, they will likely experience this at some point.

An AS person might find small talk pointless; little niceties such as saying "have a nice day" seem transparent and silly or downright annoying. We don't realize that our refusal to engage in these rituals may seem offensive to others. Small talk gives clues as to who's in, who's out, who's cool, and who's popular. Most of us weren't popular in school, and it is just more of the same at work:

"When they talk about personal things, then it becomes clear who's in what clique and who likes whom. I feel it creates an unprofessional work environment."

– DIANE, MS COMPUTER SCIENCE

Socializing is hard. Meetings, particularly, are torture. Whether it is only a meeting of two, or a few, or even a conference call, these are all social situations in which the AS person may feel ill at ease. They can make us squirm and sweat bullets, especially if there is a lull in the proceedings and people are left to chat amongst themselves or if the AS person must verbally contribute.

When asked what the hardest part of working life was, they responded:

"I am completely unable to navigate small talk. I am great at introductions, public speaking, etc. I just can't seem to have a conversation that works. Worse, I am often totally misunderstood."

– WALTER, SELF-EMPLOYED, WATCHMAKER

"Socializing is a chore; a nightmare. Small talk is difficult, especially subjects such as sexuality, or personal criticism, teasing or bullying."

– JULIAN, CLERK, UK

Small talk can be something minute, like even knowing how to say "Hey, how's it goin'?" in a way that is like everyone else. Small talk doesn't have to be verbal either; things like the "high-five," or "pounding it" (bumping fists) are physical forms of small talk. Little exchanges can cause a mountain of discomfort when you don't know how to do them right. If you don't understand that, look at this word:

你好

If Mandarin Chinese is not your native language, then this symbol is foreign to you. It is the word for "hello" and is pronounced "Ni Hao." Once you learn how to recognize it, you still have to learn how to pronounce it correctly. No matter how good you think you get, people will still hear your accent and know it's not your native language.

This inability to communicate like everyone else keeps the person with Asperger's isolated. We don't understand why people who are obviously fake or false are respected over us, or why conversation that is shallow should be sought:

> **"I don't talk to people when they expect me to. People feel alienated or disrespected."**
>
> – SCOTT, 40, BORDER GUARD

> **"The job coach I saw admonished me that I should try to understand that people love all these social aspects; she even said I should "fake it" and fit in. I responded that I've survived this many years faking it as well as I can, all the time. But living life as a phony and not feeling human—these are the things everyone seems to tolerate and expect, especially at work. It hurts me. I can't keep it up."**
>
> – ALLISON

Those with AS are sometimes described as having no sense of humor. Humor is an element of small talk, a device, an icebreaker. While it *is* true that some humorous remarks may not be understood right away because we take them literally, oftentimes it is not because they fly "over our heads" but rather under our noses. We tend to prefer surreal, satirical humor that is either irreverent or intellectually stimulating. Simple, obvious humor is often misinterpreted, or takes a moment longer to click, because the AS person is overanalyzing. This can result in a very smart person appearing humorless and slow:

> "I've never really found any jokes funny that they tell; jokes that use popular clichés. Unfortunately, these abound in the workplace."
>
> – ALLISON

When an AS person tries to converse, they may end up pontificating on whatever their particular interest is, without understanding that it might be boring or uninteresting to others:

> "Just a couple days ago someone used the word diameter. I started explaining Pi and the ways it works in math; I said 'pi equals 3.141592, and circumference equals pi times diameter.' 'We don't need an education,' they said."
>
> – JOHN, 54, FACTORY WORKER

They may also use big words and speak a little more formally than is the norm. *Hyperlexia* (a precocious ability to read words beyond age and education) is often found in young children with AS (Cook 2009), and many retain a different way of speaking though they learn to pick up the vernacular to fit in:

> "I'm 33 and only in the last four years, have I got accustomed to typical small talk. I even occasionally swear here and there, though it's really not me. Having others around me feeling comfortable, makes me comfortable."
>
> – BRIAN, FACTORY WORKER

A person with AS wants to connect with others; he/she just doesn't know exactly how to go about it. But social habits can be learned. The brain creates new neural pathways over time and is constantly forming new understandings:

"The social stuff, especially small talk, got so much better after the first year of work! By all means we should get jobs where we ask clients 'how can I help you?' Talking with coworkers and clients is great practice. I am a confident person now that I've worked in this job for two years."

— JEFF, 22, STORE CLERK

But even if a person never does come 'round to the charms of chitchat, that can actually be a plus—they have more time for work:

"I work with preschoolers 12 hours a week and love not having any time for small unnecessary chatter with co-workers."

— REANNA, A MOM IN HER TWENTIES

What the employee can do:

Because of social issues and a fight-or-flight response to all social contact, it's about as challenging for most of us to work with people as it is for a person with acrophobia to get on a plane and fly. The feelings may vary in intensity, but ultimately there is a similar fear—that this is going to crash; this isn't going to work. Yet, behind the fear and the resentment, there is still a need to connect with others.

- Examine your own hostility to small talk, and the history behind it. It may be partly born out of resentment that you don't know how to do it yourself (yet).

- Realize that small talk can take the pressure off you to actually come up with something creative to say. Talking briefly without sarcasm about the weather or sports might be all that's necessary to be accepted.

- Don't judge. That's right; the same applies to you. Because you don't like "mindless chatter" and its ilk, you don't have to engage in it. But if your coworkers feel judged by you, they will not like you.

- If you feel the tone is on a lower scale than you would like, try to raise the pitch or change the subject, but do it without condescension or being pedantic.

- Adults with AS often have a do-it-yourself approach to everything, but seek help when they need it, through social-skills therapy, workshops, or books such as *The Hidden Curriculum* (Myles, Trautman, & Schelvan 2004). These will help you learn to read things like expression, tone, body language, etc.

- Many people with Asperger's find great release and validation through writing. Seeing your own thoughts expressed in words can help instill faith in your own worth, intelligence, and right to exist. Over time, your confidence will grow enough to share some of that with others.

- Don't become jaded. Life is 90% how you look at it. Yes you have AS, but you can still be in the world and be a valuable contributor to groups, conversations and your employer with your unique insights. The more likely you are to see the good in others, the more likely they will respond to you in kind.

- Christmas and other office parties or outings can be a source of angst for weeks to come. If you want to go but are afraid, it might be a source of regret if you don't try. Remember, socializing takes practice and sometimes training. Seek advice on what to wear. Don't go alone if you can help it; instead, bring a trusted friend or partner. And don't drink too much! It may loosen your tongue, but if you are prone to saying the "wrong thing" that might not be so good.

To employers and advocates:

Those interviewed for this book reported being called names like "stupid" or "useless" because of their social difficulties. Just because they cannot discuss the outcome of the Super Bowl or American Idol with any enthusiasm doesn't mean they are dim.

- Take the time to discuss what *their* interests are, or their *job*, and you will confirm your own original belief that this person is intelligent and that is why you hired them in the first place. Try to speak *their* language.

- Acceptance is key: The more we feel that we are accepted by others, the easier it is to relax and converse.

- You do not run a popularity contest; you run a business. Social skills, unless they are an inherent requirement of the position, should not be mandated. Do not place any expectation or pressure on them to be more social.

- Company fun events for team bonding will be a nightmare for them. But a person with Asperger's will feel much more at ease if there is *structure, purpose, and something stimulating to focus on,* or *a challenging activity to engage them.* Unless outings consist of an orchestra or band to watch, a science exhibit, a scrabble tournament or a race to see who can solve a Rubik's cube, they might not come. Any event where they are just meant to chat or relax will be anything *but* relaxing.

- Meetings are generally not good environments for the person with AS. If they must attend, let them contribute in writing before or after if possible.

What are your thoughts about socializing on the job and the role or value of small talk? What do you think others get out of it?

List topics or strategies you might be comfortable with to improve your social standing at work.

4

Bluntness, Perfectionism, and That Famous Asperger's Arrogance

ome call AS *bluntness* "cutting through the smoke screen." Others call it "brutal honesty." Whatever you call it, people with Asperger's have an *irrepressible urge to inform,* often without correctly anticipating the emotional reaction of the recipient. We will throw our own potential popularity out the window to promote our ideas for improvement.

Ask a person with Asperger's if they like your new suit/car/whatever, and be prepared for the truth. Ask them if they like the way you are running the business and you may get an equally honest answer. This bluntness can result in someone being offended, particularly if the receiver thinks the person with AS meant to be hurtful. Friendships and jobs can be lost over such things. It is not that a person with AS is insensitive; indeed, we can be *overly* sensitive.

And we are often devastated to find that we have hurt someone's feelings. But we are genuine people who want to speak truth, improve situations, and not play games. Why mince words?

A person with AS may also be accused of *complaining* a lot, and of being critical. Therein lies the genius of Asperger's. We are perfectionists. We will always be looking for a better way of doing something (De Vries 2007). Rather than persecute us for it, use it to your company's advantage. People with AS do fixate on things, and like perfection. So if something is less than perfect and in need of improvement we will point it out. Whether or not we do that tactfully will have to do with how mindful we are of our impact on others at the time. But since those with AS are usually pretty single-minded, we probably will be thinking about the problem or situation that needs improving rather than the effect of our words on others. If you point out to your AS employee that he/she complains a lot they will probably be shocked, for never in their mind are they complaining—they are trying to find ways of making things better and probably not just for themselves, but for everyone else as well. They think of themselves as proactive, while complainers are those who never do anything about what they critique. They may also be hurt and surprised at how they are being misunderstood. Since it is obviously quite clear to them what their intentions are, they think you would understand as well. They will be disappointed in themselves as well for not being clearer.

As mentioned, because of sensory issues, they will notice things more than an average person: temperature, sounds, lights, sensations, etc., and we will discuss these in upcoming chapters.

They are good followers if the method is right, but if they think they know a better way, then they will say so. Their insights are usually not couched in a soft bed of rhetoric, either—they usually come right out and say things like "I know a better way of doing this," or better yet, "that's a stupid idea." This is the kind of thing that gets a person a reputation as a know-it-all, but it is not for selfish reasons that the AS person will do this, it is merely to help. Society particularly expects women to be tactful, and to be aware of others' perceptions of them, but females with AS are as naturally blunt in that regard as their male counterparts, although socialization, expectation, and years of experience might make us try to be more tactful. That tends to be something we learn because we have to, not at all because we want to or because it comes naturally.

This sort of behavior has been (affectionately) referred to as "Asperger arrogance" by folks with AS, AS professionals, and everyone else in the know. It seems that this haughtiness is not entirely unfounded. As mentioned in Chapter One, a recent study by the Department of Neuropsychiatry at Keio University School of Medicine in Tokyo found that "Individuals with Asperger's disorder have higher fluid reasoning ability than normal individuals, highlighting superior fluid intelligence." (Hayashi et al. 2008) This may explain why those with AS often feel superior to those around them who do not possess the same kind of intellectual abilities. If those abilities are not recognized, it can leave a person with AS feeling unfulfilled, unutilized, unappreciated, and resentful.

What the employee can do:

- Curb your urge to inform unless you are being asked for advice or information. No one likes a know-it-all. There are some jobs where it is more favorable and appropriate to impart or exchange ideas and information, and some that aren't (e.g., a research dept. vs. Mighty Maids). While some with AS end up in more mundane positions because of difficulty keeping jobs or getting degrees, they should bear in mind that they will not be intellectually stimulated in these environments and that their unique intelligence may not be prized in these positions. (See the chapter on Education.)

- The quickest way to get your point across (to non-spectrum people) is not always to say it directly. It is sometimes more expedient to be indirect, or gentle. I have a visual metaphor that I find effective. If you shoot your words like an *arrow* (directness) at their recipient, that person will likely recoil from them. If you *gift wrap* your words (tact), the recipient will be more likely to want to accept your *package* (the point you want to make) and take it in.

- Bluntness may also, at times, be used intentionally as a way to burn bridges. If you have AS, take a moment to look back over your life and remember times when you said something blunt to someone just to get rid of them. It probably worked. How many friends do you have now? Do you want more? Do you want people to like you? If so, try to curb this tendency. Temper it with compassion. I would never ask you to tell a white lie, but the next time someone shows you pics of their new baby, think carefully before telling them that she looks exactly like Yoda.

- Curb the tendency to be arrogant. Many of the people I spoke to for this book admitted that they can be a bit arrogant. This can rub others the wrong way.

- Understand that you may have superior intelligence of one type but possibly not another. While Aspergian Pride is a great thing, feeling superior to NTs (neurotypical or non-autistic people) can be divisive.

- Look back on your history. See where taking others' ideas into consideration might have advanced your own life, and how not doing so may have caused you setbacks.

To employers and advocates:

- Your AS employee may possess a greater capacity for a type of intellectual reasoning and problem-solving than others. Use it! You have a great resource on your hands.

- Don't say they complain too much or shut out their idea because it was put across in a blunt, tactless manner. Listen to what they say, not how they say it.

- Rather than being offended and defensive, hear them out. Ask them what they would do about a situation and they will brighten up at being taken seriously rather than being dismissed. If they do have a good point, acknowledge it.

- Do not let their unpopularity sway you into dismissing their good ideas.

Practice tact in all your interactions with people until it becomes easier.

Notice what sort of results you get from your efforts.

CHAPTER

5

Blunders, Boundaries, and Emotional Detachment

The *blunder*, usually caused by bluntness (but not always), is an Aspergian specialty and part of the reason why socializing is avoided by many. They often just don't know what to say, and end up saying the wrong thing:

> "Since I have trouble reading facial expressions and sarcasm, I have difficulty discerning people's contempt for my choice of words."
>
> – HUMPHREY, UNEMPLOYED, BS

> "There are some people who respect what I do for the school and serve as mentors. They inform me of potential political blunders I may be about to make and are ready to help bail me out if I

get into trouble. It is often difficult for me to read the political wind of things."

– STEPHEN SHORE, PRESIDENT OF THE ASPERGER'S ASSOCIATION OF NEW ENGLAND, FROM "SURVIVAL IN THE WORKPLACE" (2008)

"Office politics is all about subtlety. I have little problem noticing that it goes on and I can grasp the details of what is going on, but I'm not equipped to play the game, so I get hurt by the outcomes."

– MIKE, LAW DEGREE, SECRETARY

Just as in personal relationships, professional *boundaries* can be confusing. Some with AS have a hard time learning what is and isn't appropriate to discuss with their coworkers. Saying the "wrong thing" results in the AS person being misunderstood. Being misunderstood seems to be a common torture for all of us. Another problem with the literal nature of our understanding is not seeing the various possible interpretations of what we say:

"My co-worker had a bowl of nuts on his desk. I strolled up in a dead quiet office and shouted out, "I would love to eat your nuts! Your nuts look so good!" I still have trouble with drawing lines regarding appropriate topics of conversation until after the fact, and will take the whole conversation over."

– MIA

Because we consider ourselves genuine people and value genuine-ness, we think we should be liked and respected. We believe promotions should be based upon our integrity, not our popularity:

"I despise brown nosing and refuse to lower myself to it. I will not use people as doors to get somewhere. I always want to believe that I have earned what I have and didn't sacrifice or compromise integrity to get somewhere."

– SCOTT

A person with Asperger's Syndrome will often say or do what is logical rather than what is socially and emotionally expected of them. If a person is *emotionally detached* at a time when a more compassionate, emotion-driven response is called for, it can get them a reputation as a cold fish. An emotional situation would take the AS person into territory where they cannot control or predict the outcome, and many (particularly males, since it is something of a male reaction anyway) will avoid emotional demonstrations or reciprocations of any sort.

Mix: one logical approach to life, one aversion to emotional situations, and add a dash of difficulty expressing yourself; put it in the world to bake for a few years and out comes Mr. Spock.

Yet people with AS *can* be incredibly compassionate and kind and AS does not preclude empathy (Hesman-Saey 2008). They will open doors for the elderly, give change to the homeless, rescue wounded animals, give aid to a friend in need. But there are times, when:

1. **Empathy pathways are bypassed,** due to a high level of stress or anxiety or feeling "attacked." If there is any sort of drama going on and the AS person feels like they are being accused or implicated, they may become defensive, angry, or shut down. They might not find the right words, go silent, or stutter if upset.

2. **They feel empathy but don't know how to go about expressing it.** This is called *alexythimia.* It means difficulty identifying and describing emotions, both your own and others' (Wikipedia 2008). It is a common component of AS. Reaching out to a person with alexythimia can make for some awkward moments. For example, you may be telling them about something awful that happened to you and they will point out something worse that happened to somebody else. It sounds as if they have no sympathy for you. In reality they are trying to make you feel better but are going about it rather clumsily.

3. **The situation is something they've never experienced first-hand, so they truly do not know what it feels like and cannot imagine.** This is a problem of "theory of mind"—not fully realizing that others have feelings and thoughts different than your own. If a person with AS has never experienced the death of a loved one, for example, they may really have no idea how that feels and may not be the person to turn to for soft words and kind gestures.

What the employee can do:

- Have a sense of humor … and humility. It will make getting past the blunder a whole lot smoother. A person with AS who says something politically incorrect can follow it up with "Oops, sorry, you know what I can be like. What I *meant* to say is…." And they can get out of a potentially serious scrape that way.

- If your co-workers could be trusted to know your diagnosis without using it against you, this is one of the many reasons why disclosure would be a good thing. If people don't know you have AS, they may be less quick to forgive and forget. (Disclosure is discussed at length in "To tell or not to tell.")

- Be yourself, but as far as topics of conversation go, "when in doubt, leave it out" is probably the best advice. Understand that the things you like to talk about are not necessarily the things that others do.

- Try to find a mentor, someone whom you can bounce ideas off, whether it's a brother or sister, friend, or colleague. They can help you learn the limits of social topics appropriate for your workplace. Those things may vary somewhat depending on whether you work in a coffee house or an insurance company, but there are still limits if you want to avoid putting your foot in your mouth.

- Think about the qualities you like in others (e.g., tact, humor, gentleness) and what you don't, and hold yourself to that same standard.

- Don't overcompensate by being "too nice" just to make friends if it is not sincere. That will catch up with and exhaust you if you attempt it too long.

- Accessing emotions can be learned, especially if one is supported and in a loving environment where it is safe to do so. Try talking about how you feel with someone you trust.

- Try writing down your thoughts and feelings to better understand yourself: your likes, dislikes, positive and negative thoughts, and motivations. Journal your experiences at work and in life.

- For those with spiritual inclinations, the Buddhist/eastern practice of "mindfulness" to foster empathy and compassion for others has been mentioned as a good technique for those with AS, as is the Christian "golden rule" of doing unto others as you would have done unto you.

To employers and advocates:

- Don't take it personally if your AS employee says something insensitive. They are compassionate; they just don't know how to show it sometimes.

- They may just have an excellent point if you can overlook the delivery.

- Be patient and have a sense of humor. The brain is a flexible organ and is constantly making new connections and experiencing revelations. Social skills can be acquired, at least to some extent.

- If you don't have the time or desire to mentor this employee, perhaps someone in the office, someone who has an abundance of people skills and tact, and who is completely *nonjudgmental,* can give them a few pointers.

- If they have been a bit callous, or un-empathetic, take them aside and give them a working example or anecdote they can *relate to* rather than telling them how they *"should"* feel.

- If they are about to make a political blunder, try to explain the possible consequences logically, as if discussing future chess moves, rather than making them feel bad or inept.

Think about why you feel compassion towards a film
or other fictional character but not a real person.

Who is more important?

CHAPTER

Please Do NOT
Fill in the Blank

motional detachment doesn't just extend to words; an AS person's facial expression may be blank at times. Their face won't always match the way that they feel; nor will their expression be what one might expect in a given situation. This is a hallmark of Asperger's Syndrome and is part of the diagnostic criteria for AS:

> … marked impairment in the use of multiple nonverbal behaviors such as eye-to-eye gaze, facial expression, body postures, and gestures to regulate social interaction. (APA 2000)

"My facial expressions don't always match the way I'm feeling."

— SCOTT

Having impaired or limited facial expression does not mean a person with Asperger's is *always* blank, they may at times be quite animated, or have a beautiful smile that lights up a room when they show it, but its appearance will be unpredictable. Not receiving the facial response we expect from another can be confusing and disconcerting. We might be tempted to try to figure out what they are thinking.

- An AS person may just be lost in their own thoughts.
- Sometimes they don't smile because they aren't aware that it is the appropriate response.
- It could also be anxiety, which comes with the territory of autism.

Pointing out the AS person's unusual appearance would be counterproductive:

> **"They would all make comments about how I looked. I hated it, and I would find it hard to look happy for the rest of the day. Of course, that would bring more difficulties, because they would now ask "why do you look so sad?" till it was time to go."**
>
> **– BEN, 33, MA SPECIAL ED**

"Limited facial expression" is not going to apply to all people with AS at all times. We do not have physically paralyzed facial muscles, and we can learn to manipulate them just like any other muscles. Seeing frequent images of ourselves, now made possible with the proliferation of camera-phones, webcams, and digital cameras, can be very helpful to that end.

Facial recognition: People with AS have a little bit of difficulty immediately recognizing faces—even close friends, family, or partners. The usual flicker of recognition in the eyes, the smile, those things may be missing when they see you. They may look at you blankly for a moment, even several moments, before they realize who you are. By then they may be too embarrassed to say anything. This can be perplexing; you may think they have forgotten you; you may assume that they don't like you, or are giving you the brush-off for whatever reason. This is not the case—there is a delay in

assembling the details of the face and matching it with the person's name and identity.

Eye contact: Many with AS do not make or hold eye contact easily. Avoiding someone's gaze is traditionally thought of as being indicative of guilt or lying. (It can also show a lack of confidence, a mortal sin in a culture that currently prizes confidence over substance.) For the person with Asperger's it is an aversion to sensory input. Making eye contact has been described by some as physically hurting them, being confusing, or containing too much information. As a result of not being able to make eye contact, others may form a low opinion of this person, particularly if they are unaware of their condition, or they don't have an understanding of AS. They/you might assume the person had something to hide. The person with Asperger's often gets a bad rap because of this. They seem guilty. If you do catch their gaze (or take their picture) they might look like a deer caught in headlights.

When asked what the most difficult part of office/warehouse life was:

"Social gatherings. Having people sing "happy birthday to you" when you can't meet their gaze. People joking but you don't know when they're joking and when they're serious."

— GAVIN, MS, AERONAUTICAL ENGINEER IN HIS THIRTIES

"I know I come off as blunt and arrogant, and I really try to be careful. I have trouble with eye contact. After a little while, I guess I just don't seem that likeable, or a little unusual. I don't seem to have much in common with other people."

— WALTER

Body language: People with AS may have many other body language anomalies—an unusual way of walking, poor posture, and hunched shoulders when tense. These stem from a combination of anxiety, not being aware of how others see them, and naturally low muscle tone.

Some also have tics that can appear in times of great stress or excitement, e.g., eye or mouth twitching, stuttering, and hand flapping. These are usually brief and often barely noticeable. Stimming is something a person with AS does and it bears mentioning here. Stimming behaviors (short for self-stimulatory) can sound quite bizarre to a non-AS person but they are merely soothing behaviors, such as rocking, humming, etc. Most adults with AS can and do control stimming behaviors in public, but it may be difficult for them. It is an anti-anxiety mechanism, and repressing it, some claim, doesn't allow them to alleviate their anxiety and consequently does them harm. Having a private workspace would help, and the next chapter ("Quiet Please") addresses that issue.

What the employee can do:

- Think about how others' facial expressions affect or impress you. Do you like it better when others smile or scowl?

- For those who struggle with expression, practice. Look in a mirror. Take pictures of yourself. See the many different looks you possess and which are more pleasant, receptive or welcoming. This is not about pleasing others or being false or superficial, it's about putting your own best face forward. By using our camera-phones, video/digital cameras, webcams; and sites such as Facebook and YouTube, we can see how we look to others and learn to manipulate our expressions and appearance with a little practice. These tools are invaluable, and we should take advantage of them frequently if possible.

- Practice making eye contact a little at a time until you get more used to it, but don't over-do it. One person interviewed had a ten-second rule for eye contact and that could be far too long for some situations; and counting would distract from the thread of conversation.

- Monitor your facial expressions throughout the day. Ask yourself "what sort of image am I giving off at this moment?" Maximize your chances for social success by appearing as happy and confident as you can.

- Speaking from my own experience, I used to scowl a lot when I didn't know I had AS. It was because I was uncomfortable, unhappy, or overwhelmed in a situation and didn't know why. Now that I do know, I make a conscious effort to manage sensory overload and stop it before it reaches crisis point.

- If you don't feel happy and confident, smiling when you're down actually raises your mood, but it has to be a genuine grin. A false or insincere smile will do nothing for your mood, so keep a specific set of happy or hilarious memories in your mind, comedies in your DVD player or use Youtube to pull up quick clips that really tickle your funny-bone, e.g:

"She turned me into a newt! I ... I got better."
— JOHN CLEESE, *MONTY PYTHON AND THE HOLY GRAIL*

To employers and advocates:

- Don't tell someone to "smile" or "cheer up" if they seem down—we don't change moods at someone's command.

- The AS person will not want to inflict their mood on others. If they look a bit glum or tense, don't point it out. It will make them feel worse.

- Use positive reinforcement. We are all vain creatures. Tell someone they have a nice smile (or good posture) and they will probably use it more often or with more confidence.

- Try saying something funny or engaging. Rest assured that lowest common denominator jokes will probably not fly—there seems to be a pretty general consensus among those interviewed that cruel or clichéd humor doesn't work on them.

- If your AS employee cannot make or hold eye contact with you, do not for a moment think that means they have something to hide. It is merely something that makes them uncomfortable. Don't force it; let them be.

- Telling someone they have nice eyes sounds flirtatious, but if in an appropriate context, it can give a little confidence with regard to eye contact.

- Give them an activity to focus on to get them out of their rut. If you want to talk to them about what's on their mind, do so while engaged in an activity together, rather than just having "face time."

Practice eye contact for a day and journal your thoughts and reactions to it.

How does it feel and why do you think that is?

Are you a confident person?

If not, why not?

What can you do to improve your confidence?

CHAPTER

7

Quiet
Please

nvironmental sensitivities, or sensory processing issues, are part of the autism package deal. It is not because of a problem with the eyes, ears, nose, etc., but with the brain itself. Everyone on the autism spectrum has sensory issues and in some cases they are extreme. Sensitivity to sound is particularly common. Loud noise can feel like a physical assault but even quiet sounds may be painful and annoying, such as the hum from fluorescent lights, refrigerators, ceiling fans, printers, and other equipment.

Over-stimulation from noise in the workplace, from too much conversation, chatter, machinery, alarms, announcements, computers, etc., creates confusion. It can cause people with AS to become cranky or withdrawn; cause headaches, and trigger reactions such as having to cover one's ears; an urgent need to flee the room; feeling frozen or inert; or feeling sick, even feeling as if one's head "would explode." Many with AS don't like shouters—people who talk

louder and more boisterously than a situation calls for—and many of us are very soft-spoken.

> **"I get distracted easily by loud noises. I get intimidated when people talk too loud."**
>
> – BEN

> **"I can be traumatized by loud sounds such as a metal office cart going by. I can be startled quite easily in the office due to my auditory issues."**
>
> – MIA

Being distracted by noise is a common complaint in the workplace for all, but it has added effects for those with AS:

- Researchers have found that when people are trying to have or follow a conversation in a noisy environment, the brain "juggles" the different possible meanings of a sentence until it decides which is the most likely. This is based on context, probability, and prediction (MRC 2007). The AS mind is perhaps less likely to predict where a sentence or conversation will go. It cannot juggle in the same way, so it gets confused. Also, many if not most with AS can focus on only one sound at a time. Noise and crowded social situations are difficult and exhausting and require extreme effort to focus.

- Many with ASDs have also been diagnosed with *post traumatic stress disorder* (PTSD) (Fitzgerald 2005). Nervous reactions to loud noise are common in autistics but are also a symptom of PTSD. The person's reaction may stem from a combination of both. While some may feel that diagnoses are being handed out like candy in the current medical climate, it is important to understand that PTSD *is* often part of the legacy of a lifetime of having Asperger's.

While executives may not be aware of this, studies show that noise is the number-one complaint among *all* workers. It affects their productivity, the loss of which is far more expensive than the money saved by having "cubicle farm" offices (Young 1999). While some activities can be conducted successfully in the open–plan environment, tasks that require concentration and creativity are adversely affected; inspired thoughts go out the window, mistakes are made with data, and multi-tasking becomes difficult. Employee productivity and satisfaction decrease (Oldham, Brass 1979).

While this applies to neurotypical (non-autistic) individuals, the effect of the open place office on people with AS is even more pronounced due to sensory and social issues. When asked "If you have to work in a group or office situation, what accommodations could be made to ease the anxiety?" people responded:

"Having a quiet office; headphones don't work for me."

– DIANE

"My own isolated office, completely quiet, where nothing can be heard from outside of it."

– DAVID, 39, SELF-EMPLOYED

"The adrenalin that kicks in whenever I'm around people is exhausting and distracting. It either makes me want to party and celebrate, in which case I get over-animated and show-offish, or it makes me cranky and annoyed. If I were ever to work in an office with other people again, I would have to have a desk away from everyone, and preferably a door I could close to shut out noise and the feeling of other people being around."

– TANDY, 48, GARDENER

Many of the issues in this book could be managed more simply if the person with Asperger's had their own office or private workspace. Whether because of noise, lighting, visual overstimulation, or socializing, a private workspace is high on everybody's wish list.

> **"I would need an environment where I would have limited distractions."**
>
> – MIA

> **"Open plan offices over here [in the UK] rarely even have partitions between desks. Doing skilled technical and analytical work that requires focus and concentration in such an unnatural environment drains me emotionally and mentally. I can focus on such work for long periods, but in an open-plan office [of NTs] there are social expectations. The work I do could easily be done in a solitary office away from what are unnatural and unnecessary distractions, and with greater utilization of my skills and more productivity. Unfortunately, lack of understanding about Autistic Spectrum conditions leads employers to the conclusion that the typical modern open-plan office environment is right for everybody."**
>
> – DR. G, PHD PURE MATHS, MS COMPUTER SCIENCE, SELF-EMPLOYED

As mentioned, a person with AS can focus on a project or task for very long periods of time. Some can indulge in their passions tirelessly, but many can also devote the same rigorous hours to menial, mindless tasks with the same attention to detail. You can be sure that if they are "in the zone," they are unsurpassed in diligent effort, research, problem-solving, and just plain *work*. Having a space away from prying eyes will ensure that this goes uninterrupted. You don't want to stop the flow. They will give more time and attention to detail than anyone, but *not* under scrutiny. This is an important point and has a whole chapter devoted to it. See the chapter, "Trust Me, I Have Asperger's." We'll talk about visual over-stimulation and other sensory issues in the next chapter.

What the employee can do:

- Ask for a quieter workspace. Whether or not you wish to disclose AS outright, you can simply tell your employer that you like to give the job your best and would be able to function better in that environment.

- Try using earplugs or headphones if your job allows. No matter what you like in your off-time, instrumental music or nature sounds (wind, water, birds, etc.) will probably be more conducive to concentrating on work than music with lyrics. Save the heavy metal for the drive home or on your break.

- There are software programs you can find and run on your pc that provide the necessary sounds for white-washing environmental noise.

- If you work with a shouter, you may have to get creative. If you haven't disclosed AS, you could try telling them that you have ultra-keen hearing and that they need to speak softly when they are around you. It's a little naughty, but better than the alternative of having a meltdown.

- There are different therapies and techniques that have been shown to be effective, especially if you have a particular "trigger"—e.g., a fire alarm or siren. They usually involve playing back the sound and controlling both the timing and the volume yourself.

- Stress and sensory overload should be looked at as a whole, a "total load." You need to do all you can to keep yourself well and happy, for when your endorphins are up, you're less sensitive to pain.

- Learn and use stress management techniques: meditation, mindfulness, yoga, and focusing exercises.

- Soothe shattered nerves with natural remedies like Valerian, or chamomile tea. Don't over-caffeinate yourself.

We'll give more suggestions for soothing and strengthening nerves, and dealing with visual over-stimulation and other sensory issues, in the next chapter.

To employers and advocates:

Open-plan offices were first introduced in the 1920s, to get as many desks as possible into as small a space as possible, thereby saving money (Caruso 2009). The open-plan workspace is anathema to people with Asperger's Syndrome. But non-autistic people aren't overly fond of it either. Studies show that it is making employees sick:

> Employees face a multitude of problems such as the loss of privacy, loss of identity, low work productivity, various health issues, over-stimulation and low job satisfaction when working in an open plan work environment. (Oommen, Knowles, Zhao 2008)

Provided you haven't been convinced to abolish your open plan,

- If there is a small office that is unused, let your AS worker have it, even if they are doing the same job as everyone else. If others complain or wonder why, remember that your employee confided in you and you owe him your discretion. It is not necessary to tell co-workers he/she has Asperger's; simply tell them that this employee needs it for physical or sensory reasons. If a separate office or room is not available:

- At least make sure they have their own cubicle with tall partitions, which is created easily enough, and preferably a window, in the most quiet, private space available.

- There is also the possibility that at least some of their work, if not most of it, can be done from home. This is discussed at length in the chapter, "Trust Me, I have Asperger's."

- The advantage to the employer? You will have a healthier, happier worker, whose productivity and longevity will be increased. You will also feel good about yourself knowing that you have put human needs first.

What noises set you off?

What steps do you currently take to deal with them?

CHAPTER

8

Visual Over-Stimulation and Other Sensory Issues

isual over-stimulation is a distraction from concentration and evokes the same sort of reactions as over-stimulation from noise. But the source might surprise you. Even fussy clothing moving around can be a visual distraction, or too many people in the room, or too many machines with moving parts. For those who work outside, a windy day is a triple-threat—with sound, sight, and touch all being affected. Cars moving, lights, signs, crowds, all this visual chaos can exhaust the AS person. Back in the office, too many computer screens, especially older ones with TV-style monitors, and sickly, flickering, unnatural fluorescent lighting were both high on the trigger list. The trouble with *fluorescent light* is threefold:

- *Cool-white* and *energy-efficient* fluorescent lights are the most commonly used in public buildings. They do not include the color blue, "the most important part for humans," in their spectrum.

- In addition to not having the psychological benefits of daylight, they give off toxins and are linked to depression, depersonalization, aggression, vertigo, anxiety, stress, cancer, and many other forms of ill health. It's true. There's an EPA report to prove it (Edwards and Torcellini 2002).

- Flickering fluorescent lights, which can trigger epileptic seizures, cause strong reactions in AS individuals, including headaches, confusion, and an inability to concentrate. Even flickering that is not obvious to others can be perceived by some on the spectrum.

Natural light, on the other hand, is a natural antidepressant. It improves mood, raises energy and meets our need to connect with our outside living environment. The body uses light as a nutrient; natural light stimulates essential biological functions in the brain. It also cuts down on energy costs (Edwards and Torcellini 2002). Prior to the 1940s, natural light was the primary source of light in office buildings; artificial light merely supplemented. Now, electric lights meet most or all of workers' needs. Doesn't sound so good for our health, does it?

High on the AS wish list? A desk/workspace by a window. In addition to natural light, this also supplies a view: a place to focus eyes and mind; a mini-break from sensory overload.

Fresh air is another common workplace wish:

> **"I don't eat during the day so I could take ten-minute breaks throughout the day instead of one long lunch. That way I can clear my head and get some much-needed fresh air."**
>
> −TOM, 24, MS AERONAUTICAL ENGINEERING

> **"I would like windows which I am allowed to open any time I want. I hate air conditioning. I need fresh air once in a while."**
>
> − FUMIRO, MALE IN HIS TWENTIES, JAPAN

According to an EPA report, in the 1970s "national energy conservation measures called for a reduction in the amount of outdoor air provided for ventilation (from 15) to 5 cfm per occupant. In many cases these reduced outdoor air ventilation rates were found to be *inadequate* to maintain the health and comfort of building occupants" (1991). While standards have been raised back to 15 or 20 and even higher, new and existing buildings often do not meet these standards. The use of chemicals and an inadequate supply of fresh air is linked with *sick building syndrome* (SBS) and has caused billions of dollars in lost productivity. While we cannot delve too deeply into the causes and solutions to SBS here, minimizing the use of chemicals, getting HVAC systems checked, and increasing availability of fresh air can only be good for all workers and mean less sick pay to dish out.

Reasonable temperatures also made it onto our wish list. Since the invention/introduction of AC and central heat into the workplace, the average indoor office temperature has decreased in the summer months to the point where it is necessary to wear a sweater; and increased in the winter months to enable wearing a t-shirt. This goes against the body's natural adjustment to seasonal climate changes and evokes strong reactions from logical, skin-sensitive Aspergians. Incidentally, it also coincides with the rise of obesity in America (studies have shown that the body expends less energy in climate-controlled indoor environments).

Smells and chemicals: Chemical sensitivity has its own syndrome now, but those with AS seem to have it as part of their package deal. If you go by what most credible AS researchers believe, autism is brought about by a combination of genetic factors and *environmental insults*, such as toxins. Most with AS whom I've spoken to gravitate toward natural products, natural fibers, natural scents, etc., and have a strong reaction to smells, either favorable or unfavorable. Most furnishings made today have toxic chemicals such as fire retardants used in their production. A conversation with a scientist at the UC Davis CHARGE study revealed that bromated flame retardants as well as chemical-based cleaners and air fresheners are being looked at as some of the *possible* environmental causes of ASDs. Until we

know more, keeping chemicals to an absolute minimum in our environment would be ideal, not only for those with AS, but for all workers.

What the employee can do:

- Ask for a spot by a window and open some blinds.

- Ask if there's a way to improve lighting; e.g., if the office can make the shift to full-spectrum light. If not, ask if the fluorescent lights over your desk at least can be turned off and/or if you can bring your own lamp or bulbs.

- Wear a hat with a brim to counter the effects of overhead lights. It can also give you a feeling of security.

- Dark or colored lenses, whether cheap sunglasses or specialty Irlen lenses, can help with visual problems such as flickering and glare from lights, pc screens, and printed paper.

- Change the color in the background of your pc screen.

- Flat screens and laptops are far less taxing on autistic or sensitive eyes than old-fashioned monitors. Ask to switch if you have the old style.

- Hyperfocus in a setting rather then taking everything in all at once.

- Hang pictures in your workspace or locker of whatever appeals to you, e.g., a calming nature scene, photos of happy times, or pics of your dog.

- Have a bag of tactile tricks; things that appeal to your senses and calm you: e.g., squishy toys; a smooth rock; velvet, or a piece of fur; a rubber ball underneath your feet or between your knees that you can squeeze.

- Smell is a powerful sense that can evoke emotion. Bring flowers to work. Incense or candles might be off-limits in your workplace but there are flameless candles, potpourri, and perfumed sachets you can use instead. Those tend to be artificial, but there are spray mists made from essential oils such as lavender that contain no chemicals. You can find them in your health food store or the organic aisle in the supermarket.

- Get creative with your sensory breaks. Go to the restroom, close the door, turn off the lights, put your hands under hot water. Step outside for fresh air.

- At home or in your off-time: bathe in the dark, get deep pressure massages, whatever it takes to de-stress.

- Bring a massage pad for your chair.

- Ask for a desk away from heating or AC vents.

- Keep your own body as healthy as you can; get as much fresh air and exercise in your off-time as possible.

- Keep layers of clothing available to keep your body temperature in its comfort zone.

- You could get a doctor's note, but be warned: One person interviewed got such a note from her doctor saying she needed accommodations such as fresh air and quiet, but her employer ignored it. These types of accommodations may seem difficult and petty to those who don't share your sensory issues.

- *How* you ask for something is often more of a factor in whether or not you get it than *why*. Increase your chance of being heard by being tactful: ask for what you need in a positive way, or your requests will be seen as complaints rather than as something rational and logical.

To employers and advocates:

- Daylight and fresh air are basic human needs and just good common sense.

- At least open the blinds if you can't open the windows. According to a report prepared by the US Dept. of Energy (2002), "The comforting space and connection to the environment (from daylight) provides benefits as significant as the energy savings."

- Install full-spectrum fluorescent lights, the only electric light that includes the color blue in its spectrum. They cost more to purchase and to use than compact FLs but the benefits in terms of health and productivity should more than offset the cost. Think fewer sick days and an overall improvement in attitude.

- Regularly get your HVAC systems checked for mold and bacteria.

- To decrease energy bills and increase the energy and well-being of staff, obey inherent seasonal changes in temperature,.

- Allow the AS employee to have their own space with some control over their environment.

- If you are in the market for a re-decoration or are looking for a new space, keep the health of your employees in mind. Chemical-free furniture and fabrics are out there if you ask for them.

Using the previous two chapters, formulate a specific plan for minimizing visual, auditory, and physical sensory issues to improve your work life.

CHAPTER
9

Trust Me,
I Have Asperger's

nternal motivation is what will drive a person with AS, the feeling of a job well done, more than prestige or promise of reward. Some have done jobs beneath their level of skill or for very low pay because it simply felt good to do the work. In addition, People with AS possess a *diligent, perfectionist attention to detail*; these two factors will ensure that as long as your AS employee knows what you want or need, you can trust them to do the job right.

> "I like service and doing for others. I don't like just doing anything just for a job. I have to do more, be more, and contribute more. But perhaps I should have been more conscious of choosing jobs that would actually pay more. I worked hard for very little return because it felt good."
>
> – SCOTT

People with Asperger's need *clear instructions* from their supervisor. Note-taking or drawing diagrams in order to remember verbal instructions is helpful, if not crucial. An Aspergian needs to know exactly what is expected, including any hidden expectations or special conditions. They need to know when it is needed by. They flourish if they can accomplish it in their own way, and at their own speed, without being scrutinized. When asked what they needed from their boss:

> **"Explicit expectations with clear instructions; being able to organize my work the way I need to in order to do it. A structure within which I have the autonomy for creation."**
>
> **– ALLISON**

> **"Clear written instruction, clear feedback, and appropriate time to review and learn things. I would need an environment that would not be so fast paced that it would feel like I am running non-stop without a breather."**
>
> **– MIA**

Deadlines are a necessary part of life and are part of the aforementioned structure, but for a person with Asperger's there may need to be some flexibility within time frames. Sometimes a person with AS needs to think about an idea or project for a while first, before he/she tackles it. If you force them to dive into a task without giving them a chance to digest the Big Picture—where all the parts fit and what the outcome will be, they might not "get it." As stated, people with AS have average to above-average intelligence but the pathways to comprehension are different—things that are quite difficult to others may be understood immediately, while things that are obvious to non-autistics may take longer for the AS person to comprehend.

While some of us can multi-task, many cannot and need to apply systematic focus:

> **"I can handle just one task at a time and need enough time to get used to the routine (if there is one)."**
>
> – BRIAN

Down-time is necessary to proper functioning. There are times that an Aspergian needs to tune out both the outside world and the thoughts in their own head. In other words, do nothing. Because of sensory issues, people with AS need to stop, or limit, sensory input from time to time. This can be accomplished through periodic breaks throughout the day, in constructive use of time spent out of work, or in flexibility from the employer as to when and where the employee works.

Being trusted vs. being scrutinized impacts a person's confidence and social skills. Trying to relate to customers and coworkers is easier when one is not being watched like a hawk:

> **"I catalogued ancient Native American artifacts. I worked alone, I could go outside, I could set my own hours/pace, and I was trusted to do the work well. Heaven! On my own I can do things that make me feel smart and capable. I fall apart under the stares of judges."**
>
> – ALLISON

> **"Bosses do not seem to trust my abilities. They seem to pass judgment upon me based on something other than my performance. The less they trust me, the less I like working with them. The less I like working with them, the less they trust me. It becomes a death spiral."**
>
> – HUMPHREY, BS, UNEMPLOYED

Flexible working arrangements: Flexible Hours/Telecommuting

Depending on the type of business or the type of position that the Asperger employee occupies, an employer should consider the possibility of allowing them to telecommute. With modern technology, many jobs can now be done from home. While this might be something the employer has not considered before, with traffic, the price of gas, the cost of office space, and energy bills, there has been a strong trend among larger corporations to allow some workers to telecommute (Fawcett 2004).

> "Plenty of the work that I do can be done from home. With faxes, phones, internet, etc., there is almost no need to have an office for some businesses."
>
> – DR. G

If there are concerns that an employee would not be doing his job, there should be solid evidence to show whether or not this is the case: tasks/projects/etc. will either be done or not. But that would likely not be an issue where an AS employee is concerned:

> "I often spend a great deal of time to get things perfect, and the extra time is often uncompensated. I just love it. Also, I don't have to deal with co-workers and I control the environment. I turn on some music, go to work and sometimes five hours will go by and I will think it was only one hour."
>
> – WALTER

It would also be ideal if a person with Asperger's could work *when* they want if there is no need to force them to work within a strict timeframe (e.g., nine-to-five). While there is still not a lot of research on this, it is believed that many people with AS suffer from *sleep apnea*: difficulty falling asleep, staying asleep, and keeping regular sleeping hours. While sleep disorders are not confined to the spectrum population, those on the spectrum seem likely to

have them (three out of four interviewed for this book). Flexible working arrangements (FWAs) regarding either hours or working from home at least some of the time would ensure that they could stay productive:

> "My ideal boss would be easy to talk to, understand me, and let me take flexible hours."
>
> – DIANE

> "My issues are usually sensory, and the imperative need to actually be at work for a set period of time. I dread things that I have to do. I will usually do things I need to as long as they are not time sensitive."
>
> – TOM

Many with AS do work long hours, some virtually every moment of their day, including weekends. Even the unemployed people interviewed for this book kept constantly busy with creative projects and potential business endeavors. These included art, music, writing, invention, mechanics, software development, and more.

What the employee can do:

- Being able to work from home is grand, no doubt. And I highly recommend asking for flexible working arrangements if you can get them. But as long as you are an employee you may still be required to go in for meetings, or to participate in conference calls. Take it from one who knows; you can still feel the same discomfort at phone meetings and you can still say the wrong thing. And you will still be scrutinized at those times, and your participation judged and rated. Another downside to working from home is that it doesn't give you the social interaction and practice you may crave and require. But it is a great potential solution to many of the issues in this book

- Be mindful of the times you are under scrutiny. Practice projecting confidence, not annoyance.

- You can ask for more autonomy, but how you ask will affect whether or not you get what you need. For example, saying "I don't like being watched" under your breath while avoiding eye contact will make your superior question what you have to hide and probably result in your being watched a lot more. Try smiling and making momentary eye contact and saying "If it is all right with you, I'd like to be given a bit more trust. I have a hard time being watched when I work (interact with customers, etc.). It makes me shy and self-conscious."

- Disclosure may help and will be discussed at length in its own chapter.

- If you are not self-employed, you have to take instructions from your boss or supervisor, and listen to someone else's way of doing things. Imagine that you owned the company. You would certainly want your employees to do things your way, within reason, would you not?

- Following instructions, and taking direction does not mean you are subservient; it means you are reasonable and willing to learn. While the phrase "team player" is not normally identified with Asperger's, you can certainly understand the benefits of cooperation in theory; try putting it into practice. For a visual metaphor, think of rock climbers or trapeze artists who work in pairs or teams, in which their very life may depend upon trusting the skill of another.

- Difficulty sleeping regular hours is common and requires a combination of discipline and relaxation aids and techniques to overcome. There are plenty of non-pharmaceutical, non-addictive sleep aids available, many of them cheap or free. They include: melatonin tablets or other natural sleep tabs (available at health food stores, the organic section of your grocery store, or in the natural supplements section in drug stores), chamomile tea, lavender scent, and nature sounds or soft music. Do not keep a television or computer in your bedroom; the temptation to use them, as well as the frequencies given off by electronic equipment, can keep you awake. Get plenty of physical exercise and lots of fresh air.

- There are various types of therapy that we can undertake to deal with any or all aspects of AS—from social to sensory. Success with such therapies will depend upon a few factors, but may be worth pursuing if the practitioner is well-versed in ASDs, or if the method is specific to spectrum disorders. Research your options, be proactive, find something you can have confidence in.

To employers and advocates:

Britain's *Employment Act 2002* gave certain parents the legal right to ask their employers to seriously consider flexible working arrangements pertaining to both hours and location (when and where they worked). It is probably a matter of time before this law extends to certain individuals such as those with AS. In the US there are currently no laws requiring companies to consider flexible work, but many companies are offering it to valued employees because of its *mutual* benefits (Kelly & Kalev 2006).

- Consider allowing your AS employee to work from home. While not possible for all, with technology as advanced as it is, many jobs can comfortably and effectively be conducted outside the office. This saves the company money on office space and energy bills, and possibly even on salary (the employee will need to spend far less on fuel, parking, tolls, office clothing, lunches, etc.). This one change could solve virtually every issue in this book; it is changing the job to accommodate the human rather than vice-versa.

- If it is possible for an employee to work flexible hours, allow them. As long as the work is getting done on time, does it really matter if business is conducted nine-to-five?

- Give clear instructions and deadlines, then just let them get on with it in their own way and at their own pace. Do not micromanage time spent.

- Don't talk down to an AS employee. Most of us are very smart; our slowness at picking up certain things usually comes from *over-stimulation or sensory processing difficulties resulting in confusion,* and a *tendency to overanalyze.*

- When giving instructions, do not be pedantic or have a "my way or the highway" attitude. Lead and challenge rather than dictate.

Are FWAs possible for the current position?

Why does scrutiny make you uncomfortable?

CHAPTER

10

Polyester Prisons, Neck-Tie Nooses, and High Heeled Hell

eing aware of what we look like to others does not strictly relate to our facial expressions or demeanor—for some, especially when we are young, hygiene, neatness, and just dressing attractively can be a problem. This can have an impact on being bullied and most of us do decide at some point to make an effort to work on our personal style. We learn to find things that are comfortable *and* look good. By the time a person with AS reaches adulthood, and sometimes much earlier, they seem to have a good sense of what they do and do not like, can and cannot wear. This comes from trial and error—a lifetime of trying clothes that were uncomfortable, or styles that were fussy and distracting. People with Asperger's will put comfort and practicality before style and conformity, every time. This does not mean that your male AS employee will turn up

in sweats or your female in a hippie caftan. On the contrary; they will dress appropriately but there might be expectations in the workplace that aggravate both their logic and their skin. AS men may strongly dislike the feeling of a tie, collared shirt or stiff shoes, and prefer loose clothing with a broken-in feel. Women with Asperger's might have a strong aversion to pantyhose and high heels. The former are both uncomfortable and impractical because they don't last and are a huge waste of money over a woman's professional lifetime. These bits of attire are often spoken or unspoken requirements for office wear and again, may seem slightly superfluous to one's duties:

> **"I'm expected to wear heels at the office. I'm six feet tall as it is."**
>
> – DIANE

The need for comfort and control over the environment begins with one's own skin and is important enough to an AS person to be a factor in taking or keeping a job. Being uncomfortable would detract from their enjoyment of the work and their ability to focus. It just isn't logical to be uncomfortable all day.

> **"I'm hesitant to apply for jobs with dress codes I don't care for (i.e., suit and tie). If I take a job with a dress code, I make myself comply if I choose to take the paycheck."**
>
> – MIKE

Why a person with autism has skin sensitivity may be explained by any or all of these three factors: Some believe that autism starts with a compromised digestive system (Campbell-McBride 2004) and following that, that people with autism develop *food allergies*. This would affect all areas of the body, including the skin. *Stress*, which we know is inherent in AS, would be another factor in skin sensitivity. *Sensory processing difficulties* are part of autism, and touch is one of the senses affected.

For some, *time* is a factor. They may simply dislike spending too much of it on their appearance; a little is fine, but more than that is frivolous. For others, it is more about the *decision*; choosing an outfit is just another variable and choice they'd prefer to eliminate from their daily routine. As a result, some people with AS will love wearing a uniform because it will eliminate that whole process. Dr. Temple Grandin has created her own uniform, by wearing the same "Annie Oakley"-type shirt every day, with soft t-shirts underneath and soft trousers.

Stephen Shore, in his article "Survival in the Work Place" (2008), describes how he used to bicycle to work every day at an accounting firm. This was a logical choice: he could enjoy nature, get some exercise, and save both time and money. Perfect for the sensible Aspergian mind. Although Stephen would change into his work clothes as soon as he arrived, his employer had a problem with him entering the building wearing cycling clothes. They told him he had to stop riding his bike and start showing up in "uniform." He was let go after three months.

Looking like you belong to your tribe is an ancient survival mechanism, and the corporate tribe (or blue collar, etc.) is no different. Although costumes change and so do norms (as reflected in "casual Friday"), what attire you'll be expected to wear should be part of the decision-making process when choosing your career path.

What the employee can do:

- Don't let the idea of a new way of dressing prevent you from going for or taking a job. You can find a style that suits you, without compromising your physical needs.

- If the job you love/want dictates that you must wear a suit and tie or similar attire, know that there are alternative fabrics that are natural and comfortable. You may have to splash out a bit of money and time initially, but it is always good to update your looks.

- Real silk pantyhose are a very different experience than the usual nylon "deathtraps" as one AS woman called them. They are expensive, but do last much longer than the drugstore variety (if you can find them!).

- Open-toed high-heeled shoes tend to be more comfortable than closed-toe.

- Some dresses and suits are nearly as comfortable as pajamas.

- Have fun with dressing up. We can all get stale from time to time, and the Asperger requirement of comfort can mean that some of us would never leave our bathrobes if we could get away with it. Yet we all want to be considered attractive, don't we?

- Make a point and a plan to spend some time on a new project: your professional appearance. You might be pleasantly surprised at the results.

- If there are certain items required by your job, e.g., a uniform, hardhat or something that you find unbearable, you will have to talk to your boss to see what the alternative could be. If you don't want to disclose AS, say you have skin allergies or something similar.

- Many with AS like the feel of tight clothes with no air or fabric brushing against the skin. This is due to skin sensitivity, but loose or fussy clothing is another thing that is moving around you, another distraction. Many with AS like tight pressure on the body, but soft textures. There are things you can wear under your work clothes that will give you that feeling of security you require, such as a posture belt, shirt, or leggings. This can also help with temperature issues, as discussed earlier.

To employers and advocates:

- Customers and clients may not be as interested in seeing an office clone as you think. There is growing evidence that staff should be as diverse as a company's customer base. This makes organizations more creative and improves their profitability (NAS 2005). As long as a person is clean and presentable, allowing some personal expression might make an employee want to stick around because he/she likes it, rather than staying in it for the money. How many of us long for a little bit more freedom and self-expression in our lives and in our work?

- If you have to ask your AS employee to dress differently, please be tactful. Accentuate the positive: "you look great in a tailored suit," as opposed to "did you forget to change out of your pajamas today?"

Ideas for self-improvement.
What image do you want to convey?
What can you do to achieve that?

CHAPTER 11

A Little R&R Goes a Long Way: Ritual and Routine

or the person with Asperger's, grabbing or maintaining control over a situation is a stress management technique, for it means fewer variables will come into play and they will know what to expect. They have a plan, for the hour or the day, and if the plan gets changed by any factor large or small, they may not have a contingency plan. That's why we often don't like surprises and can sometimes react strongly to them; even pleasant ones can be annoying. If you alter the routine, we might get irritated because it means re-learning something, re-preparing. Same thing if you change the layout of the office; we might grumble at first. You also may not succeed in getting some to try food they've not tasted before, or to vary their habits. It's always good to challenge people to try new things, but it is

important to understand what's at stake—a feeling of safety and security in an otherwise anxiety-provoking world.

This doesn't mean, by the way, that we can't always think on our feet, or that we will fold up in a crisis. We may be quite cool-headed or brave in a true emergency, but move a meeting from ten to eleven and we may balk.

> **"Teaching was unbelievably difficult for me. I would get thrown off-track every time a kid interrupted. I was unable to control the class."**
>
> – BEN

People with AS require more alone time than others. This is not just to recharge their batteries; *withdrawing from social contact*, whether physically or mentally, is a control technique:

> By withdrawing into one's own thoughts, [an] individual may be limiting his environment in order to have a greater feeling of mastery. *If I don't engage with the world, then I can have control over my own small world*, the thinking may be. (Nelson 2009)

Being organized is another form of control. You know where everything is so no time is wasted on confusion, wondering, and searching. Having fewer variables means less stress. Hence the practical nature of *rituals*; some may have to eat the same foods all the time, shop at the same stores; whatever it is, it is a source of comfort and security, and one less decision to make.

> **"My worst job was working for a paint company. Every day we had no idea where we were going to have to go. I enjoy going to the same place each day"**
>
> – BRIAN

Many people with Asperger's have several self-taught skills and an ingenuity that is necessary to navigate an alien world. As a result we learn to trust and rely upon ourselves. We may be self-employed or have our own business(es) even if we are working for others. One of the downsides of working

in isolation and wearing "many hats" is that it doesn't foster cooperation or trust in the abilities of others. We need to think of people who do things we cannot, such as firemen, surgeons, or whatever, and remind ourselves that we need others.

Even though people with Asperger's like freedom within their job, they find an oasis of comfort in *routine*. They may just have to create their own to have some control over how they spend their working hours. (We talked about that in the chapter, "Trust Me, I Have Asperger's.") For those who like control do not always like to be controlled. This can translate to a need for some flexibility from the employer, e.g., the private workspace, working from home, flexible working hours or flexible breaks. As with other sensory issues, anything they can do to have some control over their world will help.

Control can be part of the *perfectionist tendency* we mentioned earlier. People with AS will want to be good at something, so they may stick with what they know they do well, or what works, rather than take the risk of trying something new that may not work.

People with AS, be warned; your need for control and rigid adherence to ritual or routine can be mistaken for stubbornness. If a person exerts control too often, it can prevent their views from being taken at face value, and from being considered seriously (a variation on the "boy who cried wolf" theme). Here is an example from my own life: My boss announced that a new technology was going to replace the current system. After hearing just a brief description of the new system I told them I didn't want to do it. I could immediately visualize potentially serious flaws and couldn't understand why they didn't see them as well. I was accused of having control issues; being lazy, and being afraid of technology. The system was implemented and I refused to use it. I turned out to be right; the whole thing was a fiasco and the company changed to yet another system, a better one, which I had no problem with. The incident, however, permanently hurt my relationship with my boss and immediate supervisor. In addition to a history of being resistant to change and exerting control, the way I communicated my misgivings: *"I don't want to do it,"* and *"it's a bad idea,"* made me appear stubborn and rude, and prevented the company from seeing the

merits of my views, even though they were correct. This was a classic combination of rigidity and bluntness and a perfect illustration of "it ain't what you say, it's the way that you say it"—that's what gets results. It is also an illustration of how those on the spectrum can be underestimated and misunderstood to the detriment of all.

What the employee can do:

- Monitor yourself. Alter your routine now and then, in any form, whether pertaining to what or where you eat, how you dress, how you look, which way you drive to work, what you do on a Sunday or before bed. Shake it up a bit.

- When you are with friends, family, even pets, watch how much control you are exercising over others. Too much rigid adherence to control can make it very difficult to maintain healthy relationships of any sort. There is a film starring Jack Nicholson called *As Good As It Gets* (1997) in which his character Melvin, an author, is a classic high-functioning Aspergian. Although it has the usual syrupy Hollywood ending, it illustrates this point beautifully and is a fun way to spend two hours.

- Do have faith in your own abilities and learn to stand your ground when necessary—but work on your style of delivery (see the chapters on communication).

- If you are in a position of authority over others, learn to delegate without scrutiny yourself; relinquish control from time to time. Use the visual analogy of a chef in a restaurant—you don't go into the kitchen to check on his work, do you? If the staff is well-trained, all will likely be well.

To employers and advocates:

- Understand that the rigidity and control that the AS person exhibits is a coping mechanism.

- Learn to discern the difference between a control issue and a good idea.

- If you are going to make significant changes, don't just throw something at them out of left field. Work up to it, and give them a little time to assimilate the new concept before the change actually has to occur.

- If they grumble at change, don't take it personally, or think they are lazy. It's just the mechanism for letting off steam and relieving the stress of having to formulate a new plan.

List ways or situations in which you can change your habits or relax control.

What was the last really spontaneous thing you did?

What happened?

Don't Tell Them Where You Heard This, But...

eople with Asperger's often become the subject of *gossip*. Their inability or lack of desire to socialize, chitchat, display all the other little emblems of normality (in speech, movement, gestures) will make them stand apart from the crowd and lead others to speculate—especially if their condition is not disclosed:

> "In a vacuum created by not having knowledge of the actual situation, speculation leading to rumors is the norm. Part of this may be the idea that speculation—feeding the rumor mill—may help flush out the truth, so therefore is good."
>
> – LEWIS

This usually starts early in life and can continue throughout adulthood, infiltrating if not sabotaging our careers, and disturbing our peace in the workplace. While a quiet, separate workspace may

keep out sensory distractions and interruptions and minimize social inter-
action, it won't prevent human nature from doing what it does:

> **"If you try to keep to yourself you still seem to stick out like a sore
> thumb and people react as if you have an attitude problem."**
>
> – DR. G.

Those with AS whose quirks are accepted by their coworkers find that they
can and do get more comfortable with each other over time, and some
interviewed for this book had been in their place of employment—hap-
pily—for many years. However, most agreed with the statement that
"familiarity breeds contempt." Even for those of us who are good at appearing normal for a while, that takes great effort and becomes exhausting. In
addition, daily exposure to others and over-stimulation tires us out; eventually we have to let our guard down and just be ourselves. As our façade
(learned behavior) begins to show holes, we begin to sense that others are
trying to figure us out; we feel scrutinized or disliked (again, over personal
things usually, not job capability) and exposed. The embarrassment this
causes, the awkwardness at being different, is a vicious cycle—the more
we retreat, the more we become suspect or disliked:

> **"I find that I can small talk with strangers better, though I often still
> come across the wrong way... it becomes a greater problem for
> me when it is people I have to be with hours a day week after week,
> because I fail to integrate socially and to relate to them like they
> do with each other. It is then that my social ineptitude becomes
> more pronounced."**
>
> – DR. G

> "Everybody's nice at first. When people get to know you or think
> they get to know you, they start picking you apart."
>
> — WILLIAM, 30, SELF-EMPLOYED LANDSCAPER

> "You don't suffer from Asperger's—you suffer from other people."
>
> — TONY ATTWOOD (2008)

Feeling uncomfortable, disliked, or misunderstood tends to make AS traits
more pronounced, and is a great cause of stress and unhappiness for most
... even if they say they "don't care." The constant struggle to be accepted,
or at least not to stand out in a negative way, affects job performance
because it saps a person's confidence. No matter how intelligent, capable,
and kind you are, if everywhere you go people misunderstand and subsequently dislike you, it will have a cumulative impact on your willingness
to even try, and will detract from your enthusiasm for your job:

> "I have the best job ever. Problem is, I'm surrounded by group-think
> types who treat me like the village idiot."
>
> — SCOTT

Telling co-workers and employers you have AS is no guarantee that they
will understand you, unless they really take the time to get to know you,
and read this or other in-depth books on AS. It is not something one can
immediately grasp, but only through a combination of frequent, prolonged
interaction, mindful observation, and study can you really acquire an
understanding of the syndrome. A popular reality television show recently
had a girl with Asperger's appearing in it for several weeks. The girl, who
was housed with several other young girls, quickly became the subject of
scrutiny, gossip, and ridicule among her housemates, even though they'd
been told she had a mild form of autism. Well, those are teenage girls, and
not mature adults right? Wrong. Young, old, educated or uneducated, gossip is built into the human genome:

"I've done a fair bit of manual and unskilled work, and I get the same kind of reactions as I get in an office, except on a more undereducated level."

– DR. G.

"small talk, jokes, attitude, expectations, one-upping, snubbing, back-stabbing, and veiled put-downs. Pretty painful stuff. I am always caught off-guard despite always being on-guard."

– RYLEE, IN HER FIFTIES, ART DEGREE, UNEMPLOYED

Females with AS, similar to their male counterparts, can have a childlike quality. It seems people often mistake the emotional naiveté of an Asperger female as flirting, promiscuity, immaturity, etc. This can and does often make her vulnerable to sexual predators and to office gossip, while she will have absolutely no idea what it is she did or is doing wrong. There is a kind of obliviousness in a person with AS, a preoccupation with one thing and an inability to grasp another, an innocence:

"I had a reputation for being a huge flirt and every guy was hot for me, and my five-year-old mind couldn't figure out why."

– MIA

Once an air of tension is created in the workplace, for the person with AS, this usually spells the beginning of the end. Many have left jobs they liked, even loved, because they couldn't get along with their coworkers. Not because they themselves caused trouble, that's the last thing they want, but because they became the subject of scrutiny and gossip and the victim of office (or warehouse) politics.

There's an inherent danger in writing this sort of book that it will seem like it's all bad news. It certainly is not:

> "I'm considered to be one of the nicest and most even-tempered employees despite being conversationally inept. Most of the time they (coworkers) accept my little quirks. I take most people at face value."
>
> – GAVIN

> "Favorite job? Being a cashier in a health food co-op, because my coworkers were all easy-going, non-critical people, some as off-beat as me."
>
> – RYLEE

What sort of environment would we like to work in?

> "A warm, laid back area. Fun people to work with that don't judge. Not having people look at you as if your head is lying on a chopping block or something."
>
> – RICK, SALESPERSON IN HIS FIFTIES

What the employee can do:

Gossip is human nature. It's always happened and it always will, until humans evolve into an entire species of saints. Meantime, how do you handle it?

- When others are gossiped about, do not pass it on. You will not be accepted into the NT gang if you gossip. And gossip can't spread if people don't spread it.

- Even if you don't gossip, you can still be gossiped about. You don't have to spread rumors to be the subject of them. So watch what you say, and don't give away your secrets/personal information. When the rumor mill runs out of grist, people will grab anything, and that will include what you've told them in the past.

- If you become the subject of office gossip, don't go to the source and privately ask them to stop. If you are alone with the person who started the rumor/gossip they can say one thing to you and then go and tell everyone else something entirely different. If they were untruthful enough to tell a lie about you, then what's to stop them lying again? Or, if they were unkind enough to talk about you in a negative way, they will twist what has been going on to their advantage once more. You've just given them more to talk about. And if you approached them in private, you will have no witnesses to back you up.

- You can try going to management, but that doesn't always work.

- Ignore it and it will go away. Maybe. But if it doesn't....

- Publicly denounce the gossip. If the rumor is a lie or false accusation, by all means defend yourself. If the gossip borders on bullying, then your job and your health are in jeopardy—we'll talk about that in the next chapter. When a significant number of people you work with are gathered together, say something like "I know that someone, I don't know who, is saying such-and-such about me. I want everyone in this room to know that those rumors are decidedly and unequivocally untrue. I would appreciate it if you hear this from anyone, not to believe it. For that person, whoever he or she is, I don't know where you got your information or what you hope to gain by spreading this malicious lie about me, but you are wrong and I'd appreciate it if you'd stop. Thank you all for your time."

  The people in your workplace may be a little shocked, but the gossip will be deflected from you to the perpetrator. You will not be fired for making a scene unless you do it in front of customers. Your boss will likely be glad you handled it without his/her assistance. Not naming the perpetrator shows a little class on your part—you don't subject people to public humiliation even if they do. Of course everyone will know who he/she is, and they will be mistrusted after that. People may already know you have AS or that you are unusual, but now they will know you are not a fool; that you have self-respect and strength. This couldn't work in all situations or for everyone, but it is something you could keep in your armory should the need arise.

- If the rumors are merely *speculation* about you, you might want to consider disclosure if you haven't already. If your behavior sets you apart enough to start tongues wagging, it might give them a frame of reference, or at least a starting point for understanding, and stop them trying to "fill the vacuum."

- It must be said: Accepting others and not picking them apart works both ways.

- Even if you ask for and get your own space, you still have to deal with others from time to time. Walls can't hold out everything, and certainly not a poisonous atmosphere. You will have to learn to stand up for yourself little by little. It isn't easy and it can be painful, so try to minimize the risk by choosing your job wisely. We'll talk more about that in the chapters on "Working with Natural Interests," "Education," and in the "Personal Job Map."

To employers and advocates:

Gossip may be human nature but it isn't our highest nature. And some gossip is more insidious than others, particularly when it is malicious or slandering.

- Discourage gossip in the workplace. If you, as an employer, let workers say negative things about another worker unchecked (provided you know about it), then you are essentially agreeing with them. You are validating their negative opinion of the man/woman. All it takes is one good soul to make a huge difference in the atmosphere.

- Speak positively to and about your AS employee. We all remember high school and how cliquish it was. There was always one person, usually a bully but not always, who had the power to make or break you, through either rejecting or accepting you. If you as a figure of authority were to say something positive about that person, such as "they are such a good worker," "they have some marvelous ideas," or even "they are the kindest person," your employees might begin to look at them in a new light. You can fill the vacuum by speaking positive truths about a person before

negative untruths creep in. But you have to do this quickly, when you see the first stirrings of speculation or ostracizing. As Winston Churchill said, "A lie gets halfway around the world before the truth has a chance to get its pants on."

- Be supportive of their efforts to join in conversations. Never laugh at someone's awkward attempts to socialize, or join in any discussion about their strange ways and habits.

- Let us not forget about the power of compassion. Suffice it to say that the person with AS is trying, and that they are probably lonely much of the time due to being misunderstood.

- The more comfortable they feel around you, the more they will open up and exchanges will be more at ease and less forced.

- Giving your AS employee their own space will minimize the amount of interaction they have to go through.

Write your own strategies to deflect or defuse gossip.
What did or didn't work in the past?

CHAPTER

13

The High Cost
of Low Behavior

ullying occurs everywhere and appears to be built into our DNA. Why should an employer take the time and effort to care? While corporations, small businesses, and the culture at large may have a "survival of the fittest" mentality, the truth is, the bully's "survival" is costing employers money—lots of money—in sick pay, high turnover rates, and lost productivity. This has come to light in recent years in studies such as the WBI-Zogby U.S. Workplace Bullying Survey (2007), which found that 37% of Americans have been bullied at work. Bullying in the workplace is defined as:

Repeated, malicious health-endangering mistreatment of one employee by one or more employees. (Namie, G. & Namie, R. 2003).

Bullying can take many forms, including false accusations; hostile words or actions; yelling; exclusion and the silent treatment; insults

and excessive criticism; and unreasonable work demands from superiors. Bullying often leads to a life-impacting decision to quit the job in order to save one's health and sanity (Keashly & Jagatic 2003).

Whether or not the target has Asperger's, bullying can cause fear, isolation, mistrust of others, embarrassment, humiliation, resentment, and hostility. It affects a person's quality of work in such ways as hiding mistakes or not drawing attention to themselves—in other words, playing it safe and medi-ocrity. This means a poorer work ethic, and decreased enthusiasm for one's job. Bullying can cause the usual physical conditions that result from stress, such as clinical depression, high blood pressure, cardiovascular disease, impaired immune systems, and post-traumatic stress disorder, to name a few (Yamada 2007).

People with Asperger's are easy targets because they are not always quick to know when they are being bullied:

> **"I couldn't always tell if another employee was doing something wrong, so I'd often tolerate it."**
>
> – BEN

Virtually everyone I spoke to for this book had been bullied in one form or another. Sometimes it gets physical:

> **"A girl at work pulled a chair out from under me. I ended up with a ruptured disc months later which neither my work nor the doctors were willing to associate with the incident. I am in constant pain."**
>
> – MIA

"I thought I was helping one guy out and he threw a stapler at me instead of thanking me. Another guy grabbed me by my tie and almost slit my throat with a carpet knife. I actually thought that he cut me. I really helped this guy out of some tight situations just a few months before this incident. The less educated and sophisticated the individual, the harder time I seem to have with them. I don't know how I could spark this sort of hatred in certain personality types. On both occasions I was totally oblivious that there was any problem, or even that I was disliked. I was blindsided. "

– WALTER

"There's usually plenty of supporting spectators and lancers, to see the matador doing what is so easy to do against the Aspergic bull. More educated people are just less direct, and less aggressive, in their delivery."

– DR. G

With the anxiety already inherent in AS, the fight-or-flight response that they innately have to social contact, and the pre-existing presence of PTSD, imagine how being bullied on top of all that must feel to the person with Asperger's. It can be traumatic to the point of serious illness and desiring to withdraw from society altogether. And of course it is usually fatal to their job, if not their entire career. This can result in highly valuable and intelligent people remaining out of work, either dependent on some sort of benefits or scraping along on incomes well below the poverty threshold:

"For me the workplace means bullying and abuse, cruel politics, isolation, scapegoating, deception, and illness. I attended graduate school but am unable to maintain employment at the minimum wage level."

– ALLISON

It is not always a co-worker who is the bully:

> "My boss at the two-way shop was hot tempered. He thought customers liked it when the manager chews out the employee; thought it proved he would take care of problems."
>
> – JOHN

> "My boss continually barked 'What are you struggling with?' whenever I needed to think. My note taking was ridiculed. I was fired after three weeks because they said I didn't fit in, they didn't like my personality, I was too slow, and I was too 'timid' with customers. Absolutely one of the most humiliating jobs in degree if not in kind."
>
> – ALLISON

> "I suffered heavy-handed posturing and veiled threats from the managers. I find it especially difficult to keep calm under pressure, and those kinds of tactics are extremely frustrating and upsetting. I cannot talk or function when I feel threatened, and I become extremely agitated."
>
> – SEAN

There are serious inadequacies in terms of legal protection for any sufferers of workplace bullying. However, if the victim has a disability, they could be aided by the U.S. Equal Employment Opportunity Commission (EEOC) or your country's equivalent. But a person with Asperger's may not be recognized as disabled if they do not meet all their state's criteria, or if they are not officially diagnosed. In addition, many kinds of bullying are difficult to prove. The fear of retaliation will keep many from taking action to defend themselves.

What the employee can do:

- Drs. Gary and Ruth Namie have started an organization called *The Work-place Bullying Institute,* which offers assistance and information. According to the Namies, there are decisive steps you can and should take to protect yourself if you suffer from workplace bullying. See the *Resources* section to get their web address.

- It is very easy, once bullying starts, to feel like a victim, to retreat, to be afraid to make things worse by creating a fuss. In my experience, and in the experiences of those I've interviewed, once the pattern starts you've really nothing to lose by doing what it takes to protect yourself legally. Remember it is your right to work without fear of physical assault and mental harassment. While our tendency is to feel flawed and that we deserve it somehow, we don't—it is purely a reflection on the people who are doing the bullying.

- Physical assault should never be tolerated, no matter what. Immediately report the incident to relevant parties—HR, bosses, doctors, or police if warranted, and probably a lawyer. Although fear of retaliation can keep us from naming names, you will *have* to or no one will be able to help you. While you cannot demand what course of action should be taken with regards to the bully, you should, at the very least, receive assurance from bosses that it won't happen again. You may have a case for compensation, but that depends on several factors, including the severity of the incident and laws governing your region.

- Be brave and as self-assured as you can be when going through such an ordeal. You have a right to a safe work environment. Do not apologize for "creating a problem"—you didn't create it.

To employers and advocates:

- Adopt a zero-tolerance policy for bullying—in action as well as speech. It's one thing to pay lip service to this policy; it's quite another to walk your talk. Bottom line, it's costing you money and making people's lives hell.

- Realize that while bullying has devastating consequences, the need is perhaps more urgent in the case of the AS person who will have a very hard time keeping a clear head during confrontation.

- That fight-or-flight reaction to social contact can also cause us to freeze like deer in headlights when we are bullied, and we may be completely unable to defend ourselves verbally or physically.

- There are organizations and individuals like myself who provide training tailored to this subject. Due to rising numbers, autism sensitivity/awareness training should soon be as required as sexual harassment training. Contact your local autism services to see if they know of any such programs or consultants in your area, or visit my web site (www.help4Aspergers.com). Management staff as well as workers can attend an in-house training.

- Places like the Workplace Bullying Institute also provide workshops and in-house training. Their contact details are in the Resources section.

- There are not enough laws against workplace bullying, but there likely will be in the near future. Get a jump on it by speaking with the bullies in your company, if you know who they are. They may be your best friends; cronies. You might have lunch together or play golf. Put your personal preferences aside, for they are costing you more money than they are worth. Tell them that their behavior towards the AS employee must stop or their time with the company will. Nothing speaks louder than that. Give him/her information about Asperger's to read, such as this book, or have them speak with an AS professional. Recommend that they seek counseling on their own, since there probably is a reason for their behavior in and of itself. You can help more than just the person with AS with your efforts. Your stance is on solid economic and moral ground.

- Follow through. This type of behavior is deep-seated and a person is not going to change overnight. Like any addict, they might backslide into their old behavior once they feel the crisis point is passed and they are no longer being watched.

- Honestly examine your own behavior towards the easy targets in your company. Has power or anxiety over pressure made you a bully? No one thinks that they are a bully, but if you are short-tempered, unfair, if you have ridiculed or insulted your employee, then you may have worn that mantle from time to time. The same advice would apply to you as to any bully: try being nice to your victim, see the positive in them, talk to them calmly and privately. Tell them that you have changed your ways. Seek help for whatever is causing you to behave in such a way. Then stick to all these things, because you will need to prove yourself over time. Once you've bullied someone, they never forget, and it will be a while before they trust you again. If this sounds like advice one would give a child, it is because bullying itself is pretty childish.

- There are many good books available to help you brush up on your leadership and management skills. You can bet that you will not find "humiliate and alienate" in any of them.

Write your own thoughts on bullying and strategies for prevention and correction.

What has worked in the past and what hasn't?

CHAPTER 14

The Power of Praise

ince we cannot always read subtle cues, positive reinforcement is necessary to let those of us with Asperger's know that we have done something well, that we're on the right track. A good supportive boss can make all the difference in the world. If your employee has done a good job on something, tell them, even if it seems insignificant to you. Praising the little things—"you are the most punctual employee we have," or "I really like the way you handled that assignment," or "the new filing system is much better than the old"—will give them more confidence. More confidence means more motivation, and a happier, more productive worker.

As any book on effective management would tell you, it is better to motivate people for the right reasons instead of punishing them for the wrong. Direction and correction are preferable to humiliation and condescension. This seems like a no-brainer, but many bosses will do the latter. These are bullying tactics (see the previous

chapter) and an employer should never think that they will achieve the desired results in the long term.

The power of praise should not be underestimated; it should be cultivated:

> While oftentimes largely ignored by managers [praise] can be an extremely useful method of giving a worker a sense of worth. It has, in countless examples, been shown to dramatically increase productivity. (HR Village 2009)

Giving rewards for a job well done *after* the fact does nothing to encourage someone along the way:

> The company must do more than look at the end result and reward outcomes. Leaders must encourage their managers and supervisors to actively engage employees during the work and positively reinforce valued behavior—in real time. (Pounds 2008)

Giving positive reinforcement is even more vital in the case of the person with Asperger's, since we tend to be perfectionists as well:

> Those with both Asperger's and perfectionism can tend to be exceptionally sensitive to criticism and suffer from the fear of making mistakes or errors. You can help them get a more realistic view of their own achievements by emphasizing what went well. Acknowledge them in a positive way all the time and let them see how great they are doing. (De Vries 2007)

"The principal rarely spoke to me, and when she did, she would rebuke me in front of the students. I find that if the boss is going to talk condescendingly to me, or scream at me (in private or in front of people), then things aren't going to be good."

– BEN

It is also more crucial because of the general feeling that the AS person has that everyone else seems to "have a script" while they have to adlib. The uncertainty that comes from this inability to read expression, tone, and body language, will be allayed by positive praise when something is done well—even the little things.

> **"I don't find much fault with my current boss. He gave me a great review last time. He says I'm the reason his store looks so good."**
>
> – RICK

If this sounds like a lot to ask, know that people with AS don't seem to have unrealistic expectations from a boss:

> "He/she would have a friendly, courteous spirit."

> "He would see him/herself as a collaborator and would not hide behind the role."

> "Someone who understood my limitations, and could make realistic challenges."

People with Asperger's who make an effort to understand the syndrome are aware of its pluses and minuses. They will come to realize that a good working relationship is a two-way street:

> "I had a perfect boss. I was the problem."

What the employee can do:

- If you find that your employer's approach to critiquing your work is causing you anxiety, you can ask him to do so in a more private and constructive way.

- Try to understand where your boss is coming from if you receive negative feedback. People with AS generally, by their own admission, do not take criticism very well. Think about your own approach to others. Often you speak your mind bluntly without couching your words in a pretty package. You expect others to understand where you are coming from: a desire to improve, a quest for perfection. Understand that your boss wants the same thing and may have his own communication issues. Try to work together to come up with a solution.

- Giving praise goes both ways. It is important to show appreciation for others' work and to be generous in your own spirit if you would like to have the same shown to you.

To employers and advocates:

- Give praise freely and frequently. These are markers that let an AS person know they are on the right road going in the right direction.

- The AS do-it-yourself ingenuity means that he/she has put some real effort into doing their job. If it has not been done to the boss's satisfaction, censure must be done privately and respectfully, not in front of customers or co-workers:

> "The managerial staff were rude, ignorant, and insensitive. And in some cases, downright spiteful. The way you are called into a room with two or more managerial staff when they wish to speak to you about concerns; it always feels like an interrogation, and I believe it is."
>
> – SEAN

- People with Asperger's are great emulators and learn social behavior by copying. If you are positive and tactful with us, over time we learn to be more diplomatic with others.

How do you respond to praise?

How does it feel to give it?

What sorts of reactions do you get from people when you are positive as opposed to critical?

CHAPTER

15

Working with Natural Strengths and Interests

ork with a person's interests to utilize their strengths. This will ensure that you reap the most benefit from your AS employee and he/she will achieve the greatest job satisfaction. Don't push someone into a role they are unsuited for. Sounds logical, doesn't it?

The things people with Asperger's don't do naturally well (e.g., *socialize*) usually fall into a realm that doesn't directly affect the job they are doing. To the contrary—sometimes their social weaknesses are career strengths. They don't like to chitchat on the job, so that means they will have more time for work. They like to focus, so they won't be flipping through magazines under their desk. If their job is research, no one will do it better, as people with AS are information addicts.

In addition to research, an AS person might excel at organizing, problem-solving, writing, composing,

repairing, designing, engineering, inventing, mathematics, and just about any other solitary activity in which they can control all the elements. Even more mundane activities like mowing lawns may appeal, or painting houses, because there is control, a definable outcome, and little interaction with people, as well as freedom to listen to music, news, or audio-books. Putting them in a position to deal with others is more problematic because people are uncontrollable and unpredictable. Some may be excellent teachers, but an AS person would likely not enjoy teaching high school, but rather, college, university, or younger elementary school children.

> **"One of the most important things is early diagnosis. I didn't realize I had AS until I was nearly 30, and I wound up going into jobs I wasn't suited for."**
>
> – BEN

It is worthwhile to work with natural Aspergian tendencies and channel them into appropriate activities rather than forcing a person to do things that will just demoralize them. Challenge is good, but as the old adage goes, you can't push a square peg into a round hole. As we will discuss in the chapter on Education, it may be beneficial to suggest or encourage additional classes if your employee's natural skills tend toward a certain area but they lack the practical knowledge or necessary piece of paper to put those skills into practice. Many with ASDs have savant talents or "obsessive" interests that could be put to good use in appropriate vocational contexts (Müller, Schuler, Burton, & Yates 2009).

Job-sharing or job-pairing can enable workers to utilize their strengths while ensuring that there are no gaps in service or performance:

> "I worked for a government corporation for a while and one boss referred to me as the 'brains' of the department. Unfortunately, the person whom I was paired with, I was driving crazy because of my oddities. This problem was solved when I was paired with another, and we were compatible. In this way we built teams of inspectors. Some combinations of personality traits and skills created well-functioning and harmonious teams and others did not."
>
> – LEWIS

One man who has a top level IT support job has done very well and was promoted to a management position. He loves his job, loves his work and has been given his own office so that he can focus, but he is expected to attend meetings, which is difficult for him. Meetings are often high-stress points for those with AS:

> "I hate meetings: I can't face the CEO properly or communicate effectively. I would love to be left alone to do IT Management and Administration and have someone attend the meetings for me."
>
> – GAVIN

The company values him enough to give him this position, but this ongoing battle with anxiety may continue as long as he is forced to attend meetings. The non-AS boss and coworkers could not possibly understand how uncomfortable these gatherings will make the AS person feel. One solution would be to let him receive the agenda in advance and to convey his contributions on paper rather than in person.

Because of the social and environmental difficulties that create anxiety for the person with AS, some have been asked by their employers to take drugs:

> "He asked if there was any medication I could take to fit in. I wonder if NTs would be prepared to take mind-altering medication so that they got on better with AS colleagues."
>
> – DR. G

As we all know, doctors are prescribing medicine (some say rampantly) to help people deal with psychological issues that prevent them from actively participating in life, e.g., depression. The reasons that people with AS do not naturally socialize well are not psychological but *neurological*, although depression can and does occur as a co-morbid symptom of Asperger's.

There is no pill to cure autism and many would not want to be cured of AS, which brings with it many gifts. While some may take medicines to offset the anxiety and other byproducts of Asperger's, it also makes sense to work with and utilize one's natural tendencies to foster a feeling of well-being and usefulness. Temple Grandin is a proponent of using a small, 1/3 to 1/2 dose of anti-anxiety or antidepressant medication and I know of others on the spectrum who concur with that. However, of all the people I interviewed for this book, only two were on antidepressants and finding them helpful. The majority had been on them at one or more periods in their life and found they created more symptoms than they alleviated:

> "I've been on Effexor, Prozac, Seroquel, Depakote, Wellbutrin, Celexa, Concerta, Trazadone, Nortryptalene, Amitryptalene, Ambien ... and more. Maximum recommended dosages on most. The last idiot doctor I had increased my dosages or added new medications about every other visit—even when I asked about other alternatives."
>
> – ALLISON

"I went through Ritalin as a child but was taken off as it didn't work. I later was on Thorazine and Tofranil taken at night to help me sleep and control anxiety. I weaned myself off them by age 13-14. Later, in 2000-2001 I got an intense technical help desk job where I didn't feel mentally adequate and restarted the med journey voluntarily, first seeking something from a general practitioner who gave me Welbutrin samples. They were horrible. I couldn't focus on anything. Then I sought an ADD (attention deficit disorder) assessment from a semi-professional, who then referred me to an ADD med man who ran me through the "try this and see if it works" gambit. We tried various combinations of common amphetamines like Adderal. I eventually rejected everything due to side effects like jitters, speeding, and buzzing. I decided, that whatever my issue, I would perform, work through it, feeling the way I was meant to: natural."

– SCOTT

I am certainly not advocating taking yourself off of medicine if you are finding it helpful and if the benefit clearly outweighs the risk. But, in this day and age of "take a pill for everything," it is important to realize that people come in all varieties; we are all part of the great balance of this world (see the next chapter on Psychometric Testing). Instead of "taking the edge off" the square peg with drugs in order to make him fit into the round hole, would we not be better off making a square hole? Employers, counselors, job coaches, and others must realize that there are people who are not suited to certain things but who are still very strong assets in the workplace. Although it is good to test and stretch boundaries, working with what a person has rather than against it, is where you will achieve your greatest mutual results. Otherwise a person is always fighting an uphill battle and will never reach their potential.

"This isn't a symptom I have, it's a skill; a skill you don't have. And because you don't have this skill you see it as a symptom."

– PHIL, FATHER OF AN AUTISTIC SON

What the employee can do:

- If you are currently employed, try to work with who you are and what you are good at. Share these thoughts with your employer as in "I really like research but I really don't like dealing with customers." Or, "I know I have to attend the meetings but I am not comfortable speaking in front of the whole group. I'd rather put my thoughts and contributions in writing to you personally."

- It's better to be upfront about who and how you are from the beginning and stress your positive points: "I keep to myself. Some might see that as shy or unfriendly but I'm a focused worker."

- Some with AS have taken public speaking courses and find it does help with giving presentations.

- There *are* holistic alternatives to psychotropic drugs. Most of these, like St. Johns wort, 5-HTP, and gingko biloba can be purchased in super-markets, health food stores and vitamin shops. Investigate natural remedies for depression, mental clarity, and anxiety if pharmaceuticals are not helping you, or if you want mood-elevators that don't have addic-tive properties. Some do interact with drugs and some can have side effects so research these as carefully as you would pharmaceuticals.

- See "The Personal Job Map" and do the exercises suggested there. This will help you to determine whether or not you are in the correct field and help guide you into your "best fit" job or career.

To employers and advocates:

- Observe and acknowledge what your employee is good at.

- Listen to him/her when they tell you what part of the job they feel comfortable with and what part they don't. Perhaps there are some things that aren't quite so necessary, especially those that involve contact with customers and co-workers.

- Don't be frustrated or think that your employee is being stubborn, unreasonable, or lazy. There are simply some things that will be hard for them. As one said, "there is a big difference between *can't* and *won't*." The more you take the time to understand Asperger's the more this will make sense to you.

- If there are some aspects of the job that stretch the person's boundaries (meeting with clients, giving presentations, making calls), try to support them in learning to do it properly (without scrutiny), or find a mentor they can work with (another supervisor or coworker) who will give them pointers and show them the ropes without being critical when they falter.

What are your/your employee's particular strengths?

What can you do to use them to your advantage?

**Examine resistance to certain activities—
is it a *can't* or a *won't* situation?**

CHAPTER
16

Conformity, Psychometric Testing, and the New Segregation

"We are unique and out of the box. We are the dreamers and the inventors. Without us the world would lose some of its music."

– MARA, 37, AS WIFE OF AS MAN,
AND MOTHER OF TWO AS CHILDREN

I think it is safe to say that people with Asperger's Syndrome are somewhat non-conformist. Social, group-think rituals like "the wave" or line dancing generally make us cringe. Think of Woody Allen's character in the animated film *Antz*. If a DJ shouts "Let me hear you say *yeah!*" to a room full of Aspergians, he is sure to be disappointed. But that doesn't mean we don't want to go to the party.

When a person tries to enter the world of work these days, they are going to find a guardian at the gate: the *psychometric test*. This, apparently, is acceptable to many people, but to Aspergians, the PT is like a bouncer at the door of a nightclub who doesn't let us in because we're unfashionable.

Psychometric tests were originally created and applied to measure intelligence. More recently they have been used to attempt to measure and quantify aptitude and personality. *Aptitude* tests usually have definite right and wrong answers, to determine if you have the correct skills for the job, for example, math skills. (This is not the same as a *Career aptitude* test.) A person with AS would likely not have any particular objection to such a test, and might even relish it.

Personality tests have been created because there is so much more to a job than just *tasks* and employers want to make sure that the person they hire is compatible and cut out for "the Team." They are usually multiple-choice with no obviously correct answer. Test-takers are often told there *is* no right or wrong answer, yet, somehow, mysteriously, they are scored on their performance. Personality tests can be given in person, online, or over the phone, where you give your answer by pressing a number.

These tests are being used increasingly by employers. They are created by various companies and sold for profit. Whether or not a candidate has AS, there is controversy over their use:

- Companies who create them are usually the ones responsible for "grading" the test and giving the potential employee's score to the employer. They usually don't tell the employer which answers are considered correct or functional and which aren't, much less the applicant.
- There are no standards for these tests monitored by any governing body.
- There is little if any proof that they work.

In *Employing People with Asperger Syndrome* (NAS 2005), the authors state that unlike a practical test which gives the autistic person a chance to demonstrate their skills and knowledge, a psychometric test would be confusing because of the lack of a concrete right or wrong answer:

The world of psychometric profiling is unlikely to be one to which people with Asperger syndrome can relate to … it would be unfair to assess them on this basis.

Psychometric tests have been highly criticized throughout respected psychology journals, with regard to both efficacy and ethics. Most human resource web sites will mention the controversy in one breath but in the next, say *"don't worry, there's no right or wrong answer, only the truth."* Following that, they will tell you how to prepare. These contradictions have an Orwellian odor and are anathema to the AS person:

> **"I have an issue with businesses expecting people to be 'robots' in any way, whether it be how people dress, their hair, etc. I feel the average corporation is like 'the Borg,' and we are all expected to assimilate, but then again, 'Welcome to society: Resistance is futile.' Businesses have so much to learn about productivity through building environments that foster a good morale through acceptance of diversity. I think we are beginning to see a taste of this, but that's probably all we will see for now."**
>
> **– MIA**

When I met Temple Grandin one of the first things she said to me was *"you have to sell your work, not yourself."* The personality test asks us to sell ourselves first, in order to be given the opportunity to sell our work. As a person on the spectrum, my own experience counts. Having taken that test only once, I will say this: I will *never* subject myself to that again. Not knowing I had AS, I felt violated and confused. I had no idea if my answers were good or bad, right or wrong, and was appalled that I would never find out. I didn't pursue that job. I stopped going into that store for months thinking that the manager now "knew" all about me.

The practice of personality testing is discrimination as blatant as a "whites only" drinking fountain. It makes no allowances for differences in thinking. It is not an employer's business what I think, only what I do, and only in the workplace.

These are the types of "Crystal Ball" advertisements companies use to sell their tests to other companies:

Predict the Success of New Hires.

Free Employment Assessment;
Know Your Employees Before You Hire.

Here is an example of a question from a personality test:

Choose one of the three words to describe yourself:

- sure

- variable

- adequate

(Carter & Russell 2001)

A person with Asperger's would likely balk at this sort of question, believing it to be illogical. It would entirely depend upon the situation; at any given time, they are likely to feel any one of these three things. During the test an Aspergian would likely feel unsure, and probably inadequate, so therefore might begin to choose "variable." Variable could mean flexible, which is a positive trait. Next we might start second-guessing and thinking that the scorer would see that as meaning undependable or inconsistent. We might throw up our hands and walk away from such a ridiculous test, and would expect everyone else to do the same.

If you study books on how to prepare for such tests, they teach you to say what people want to hear. To us, that is simply not genuine and is contradictory to their purpose.

While these tests, understandably, are meant to save time and money by increasing the chance of hiring someone suited to all facets of the position, it does not seem to leave much room for hiring the innovator, the maverick, or the creative genius. Nor does it accommodate those whose skills might outweigh any minor inconvenience of having to put up with a few idiosyncrasies; a person whose unique way of thinking might enrich others if given half a chance:

> "Being 'unique' hurts more than it helps. People with AS can adapt but will still have quirks. If employers understood this, perhaps they wouldn't dismiss us as a bad fit for the position."
>
> – MIKE

Proponents of such tests use arguments such as:

> If a candidate is nervous or falls to pieces, despite having seen examples beforehand and despite having trained personnel on hand to explain and reassure, this is a valid and pertinent indicator of that person's ability to handle a stressful situation. (Rowe 2009)

Yet many of these tests are conducted over the phone or online. This same author states that testing is necessary because people in general aren't sticking around on their jobs longer than 18-32 months—*perhaps there is a reason for this.* Perhaps instead of trying to find people that will put up with the culture and environment, the work culture and environment could be improved so that people feel fulfilled with their lives?

There is a growing outcry against the use of personality tests from several different sectors of society, including the medical/psychiatric community, civil rights groups, people with ASDs, and Autism/Asperger societies. They remind us of the importance of balance and complementary forces in our world:

> "As with male/female tasking and differentiation, Asperger/ neurotypical differentiation and tasking may be an advantage to our species as a whole. In an odd way, the 'non-social' part of our species provides advantages to the social part."
>
> – LEWIS

There is growing evidence that employing people with a wide range of backgrounds and experience can make organizations more creative and improve their profitability. Their staff should be as diverse as their customer base. (NAS 2005)

I sometimes wonder why all of the great applications around today, such as spreadsheets, email, word-processing and relational databases, were invented in the seventies and eighties. Our greatest achievement in the past fifteen years seems to have been to refine the visionary approaches of a previous generation—one that cherished and valued the creative spark, and tolerated eccentricity.

One persistent myth in the IT industry is that, in development work, we need team players, not mavericks. It depends on what the team is doing. Harmony is fine for picnics and team-bonding exercises, but is not necessarily the precursor to productivity.

Nevertheless, "Human Resources" practitioners persist in many enterprises, with their 'personality' screening. This is an evil practice. Many will have experienced job interviews for a technical role where one is required to engage in 'role play,' or is asked silly questions like 'if you were an animal, which animal would you like to be,' and so on. Any trained and qualified psychologist will tell you that the tests are bunkum.

When they suddenly pop up in an interview, without prior consent, and the candidate has to give the "right" answer when a potential job is at stake, they are a gross impertinence, and probably illegal. (Factor 2006)

Well, one could always cheat. Because of the rise in use of psychometric tests by employers, a number of books have recently been published that will introduce you to what they are all about and show you how to prepare yourself against such a test and include tips on how to relax and improve

your performance during the test—the test which is meant to be a spontaneous, accurate assessment of your true personality.

Some states have imposed restrictions on the use of personality tests. It's a start.

What the employee can do:

- Many people with AS refuse to entertain the idea of even applying to a company that utilizes psychometric tests to screen applicants. If you feel strongly in this way, at least write a letter to the company explaining why—either because you have Asperger's if you choose to disclose, or on ethical grounds. They will probably not be able to bend the rules or forego the test for you, but at least you will have had your say.

- If there's a job you want to go for that uses this method, you can purchase a book that helps you prepare.

- Accepting diversity goes both ways. Some people with AS begin to think that people with Asperger's are superior to NTs. They come to distrust the non-ASD population. This is discrimination too. If you want to be successful in this world, you must learn to accept your own flaws and acknowledge the strengths of others. Think of every encounter with a non-autistic person as a cultural exchange—of ideas, rituals, norms, phrases, etc.

- If Psychometric testing truly gets your goat, take some action and write to your favorite civil liberties/anti-discrimination organization.

To employers and advocates:

- If you already have these tests in place, you may see no good reason to remove them. Yet, if you search for evidence, you will see that there is inherent discrimination in these practices and little proof that they work.

- If you choose to end this practice, you would be on high ethical ground, and ahead of the game, for it is quite possible these will become illegal at some point in the future.

- I would also urge you to consider whether Albert Einstein (a probable Aspergian), Dan Aykroyd (diagnosed with Asperger's), or other famously successful Aspergians like Dr. Temple Grandin are worthwhile contributors to society. Do you think they would approve of, much less pass, a personality test?

Would you take a PT?

Would you prepare?

If you are an employer, what do you think are the dis/advantages of hiring diverse personality types?

Asperger's and Education: Star-Crossed Lovers?

espite a high level of intelligence and a love of information, many adults with AS had a difficult time getting through high school, much less college, due to the lack of available, correct diagnoses and understanding of Asperger's. Social struggles, anxiety, lack of interest in the subject matter, bullying, and even feeling smarter than the teacher can all play a role in preventing matriculation or completion of a course or degree. Of those interviewed, some had GEDs but went on to at least attempt college. Some had several vocational (short-term) or distance qualifications, meaning less time spent with others in close proximity. Others took longer than usual to finish their degree, needing time off because of stress. Those who were highly educated (PhDs) preferred the doctoral phase of learning because of the autonomy it afforded. Still to this day, there are very few universities that are savvy enough and educated enough

on the topic of Asperger's. Lack of resources at the universities is a big hindrance.

Your AS employee may have abilities and intelligence greater than their education would indicate. For this reason:

- They might not be at the level of pay, prestige, value, responsibility, or importance that they feel they should or could be at
- You might not be taking them as seriously as you might if they did have a higher degree
- They might be in the wrong position or field altogether.

People without degrees tend to end up in jobs that don't require them. Factory, warehouse, retail, general office and general labor positions usually don't require a degree but they often do require *people skills*—either because one is dealing with the public or with co-workers. At this level (blue-collar or lower-level white collar), a person's ability to take orders rates higher than their ingenuity. A young AS man may become a stockboy; a female may become a customer service operator … simply because they never got a degree.

Most with AS will find themselves playing roles that will inevitably involve too much exposure to people, not enough prestige, and not enough utilization of their intelligence. These bright and sensitive people become demoralized by all of the social difficulties they encounter, and all of the aforementioned challenges. They wonder what on earth is wrong with them that they cannot keep a job. They will switch jobs or even careers many times. They may also become self-employed. (While the latter has its advantages for the person with AS, it is often a financial struggle and may keep them in isolation, never really addressing the inherent need to connect.)

What can be done about this? Most people with AS love to learn. Most have average or above average intelligence, are even gifted, yet they drop out of school or university. How can this be prevented? One should hope that a high-performing student would be recognized and that their disappearance would be followed up or prevented. In high schools, perhaps now they

would, but for those who are over 35 at the time of this writing, their condition existed before the diagnosis and before proper support structures were even defined:

> "I have an Associates Degree and a diploma from a watch-making school. I originally was going to get a B.A., but dropped out after trying to function while living in the highly social dormitory."
>
> – WALTER

Even now, most universities' Office of Disability Services (ODS) have no particular understanding of AS and its impact on a student's ability to finish a degree (Farrell 2004). As a general rule, they do not have the time or resources to pay attention to whether or not one young adult has mysteriously dropped his/her classes. As a result, many students with AS just disappear, undetected. Perhaps in a smaller institution, a teacher might briefly wonder why such a bright student dropped out, but most likely would not follow through to an answer. If a student has social difficulties, it might be put down to psychological or personal issues rather than neurological; and while counseling can and does help, it is probably safe to say that unless the counselor makes Asperger's Syndrome their specialty, they can do more harm than good. They must have an in-depth understanding to be effective.

The responsibility to stay in school is entirely the individual's, rather than shared by the colleges and universities. These institutions largely don't have the budget to create a program to support the approximately one percent of the population who are on the autism spectrum. It is thought that of all those with AS, only 25 to 30 percent of them finish high school and only a quarter of those go on to college (Schwarz 2002). This statistic doesn't state how many of those actually graduate from college and at what level.

While there are programs designed specifically to enable people with Asperger's to attend university and to support them through to graduation and even on to employment, these are the exception, not the rule. They tend to be costly, and space is limited. (See "Educational Programs" in the Resource section.)

> "My husband flunked out of college or dropped out repeatedly over twenty years before he got his diagnosis. When he decided to try for a degree once more, he got an official report through the combined efforts of his doctor and a lawyer, to protect him from failing. The report stated that he needed certain concessions to help him finish. He's doing fine."
>
> **– KIM, WIFE OF AS HUSBAND AND MOTHER OF AS SON**

For most people, who have neither the diagnosis nor any such report, flunking or dropping out becomes habitual, and it is not uncommon for people with Asperger's to have two or more partial degrees. It is important to state that even those with several or higher degrees will still have problems staying in work, if their needs are not constructively addressed in the workplace.

What the employee can do:

If a degree is important to your self-esteem and to your financial prospects, you can try a couple of things:

- You can go to a university or college part-time while you are working.
- You can try online or distance learning.
- There are some universities (e.g., Empire State College in NY) that award college credit for professional and life experience to be applied towards a degree, thereby reducing the number of classes you must take to complete your degree.
- There are specific university programs for people with Asperger's Syndrome (see "Programs" in the Resource section)
- There are shorter vocational courses one can take to get professional qualifications, e.g., hairdresser, personal trainer, auto mechanic, cook, etc.

To employers and advocates:

Economics are the bottom line, and there are no economics without people. Human resources are your best resource. If your employee has AS, getting fired will only begin or add to the demoralizing string of social failures he/she may have experienced. And it's just one more body in the bread line. Further, outside of employment there are few or no other ways for a person with AS to get an income. Benefits are very hard for someone with Asperger's to acquire.

• Talk to them. Find out what their interests are. If you feel your employee is in the wrong job, or you feel they have not tapped their potential, don't just cut them loose. It might be worthwhile to encourage them to take some classes, whether directly related to their current position or not.

• You might find that their newfound confidence improves their outlook and performance at work.

• They might become promotable if the studies correlate to the job, e.g., an electrician may become an engineer.

• It may be possible to expand the duties of their current position to create something that is of more value to you and more satisfying to them. A secretary might become an accounts manager. A receptionist might design and create the company newsletter or brochures.

• If they are in the wrong field altogether, you still might encourage them to take some classes, and give them time to do it as well as time to find a new position. Wish them well. Your current janitor might become your future lawyer.

List possible strategies for continuing education
or putting what you already have to better use.

(This is explored further in the "The Personal Job Map.")

To Tell or Not to Tell, That is the Question

I f you are an employer, you may be reading this because your employee had the courage to come out and disclose to you that he/she has AS. You may be conjecturing that an employee has an ASD. Whatever the case, understand that it takes courage and effort on the part of a person to tell people that they are "on the spectrum."

There are many arguments for and against disclosing that one has Asperger's:

- Staying "in the closet" does nothing to advance the cause of and shine a positive light on those with Asperger's.

- *But:* If an Aspergian is getting along well on their job, why rock the boat?

- If a person with AS doesn't disclose their syndrome, their associates will have no frame of reference, no platform for understanding their anomalous behavior.

- *But:* If a person with AS tells coworkers/bosses they have AS, chances are people will *still* constantly wonder why they do the things that they do.

- If a person does not disclose their AS to their employer, they are not going to be protected by the ADA should they be discriminated against.

- *But:* It is still often very difficult to prove that discrimination is at the root of problems at work anyway.

If you have AS, no one can tell you what is right to do in this regard. Here are a few different perspectives:

> "I don't tell people. They are either hostile (family), suspicious (acquaintances), or patronizing (like call center workers, plumbers, etc). I've never had a reaction that didn't fall into one of those categories."
>
> – TRACY, 29

> "No cop, judge, or anyone else ever cared if I had autism or not. Why should they? They don't know what the syndrome is anyway."
>
> – FRANK, 25

> "My fear is that I will be put into a box or be thought of as someone who needs special treatment or sympathy. I simply want understanding. I struggled but am nevertheless gainfully employed."
>
> – RICHARD

"It is best to let them know what it is so they don't guess the worst. The vacuum of not being able to insert a label means others place it. While many claim that they don't like labels, labels are used because that is how people think and categorize. The term 'Asperger's' displaces 'crazy.' Preemptive strike—fill the vacuum before someone fills it for you. This is why I think it is better to tell."

– LEWIS

"When it comes to getting a job, I would not recommend disclosure. I know it is illegal for an employer to discriminate against a person with Asperger's, but the truth is you most likely will not get the job. An employer will not want to take the risk when he/she can just find a 'normal' person to fill the position. Plus sometimes with disclosure people think Asperger's means a form of retardation and you'll get treated as such. I think I should clarify that this depends on how much Asperger's affects you. For people who have an exceptionally hard time with social interaction, they might need to disclose their Asperger's in order to explain what might be seen as 'extremely weird and strange behavior.' In this case, you would not want your boss thinking you are some crazy person."

– DIANE

"I gave the store manager a copy of AS traits so that maybe he would understand some of my quirks and behavior."

– RICK

"I have tentatively told a couple of people, but stopped. I could see they couldn't understand so there is no point."

– JULIAN

"It is always a personal decision. Disclosure does not necessarily mean walking in and saying that you have AS, rather to disclose whatever facets of the AS may be a challenge to you. It may be as simple as asking the employer if it is okay to bring lamps in for an office so that the fluorescent lights can be shut off...it is more about self advocacy in general. In most cases we urge individuals not to disclose until they are hired, as it may hurt your chances during the interview process, whereas they are protected by the ADA once hired."

— MAT K., AS ADVOCATE

Those who are not officially diagnosed would not be protected by the ADA (Americans with Disabilities Act) and even if you are, it may be quite difficult to prove why you were fired.

Sometimes discrimination is blatant and justice is not done. This story comes from a man in Northern Ireland, who passed the rigorous test for selection into the N.I. Police force:

"The head of the Police college became aware that I had AS and I was terminated for 'failing to disclose my Asperger's disease'(!) The actual dismissal proceedings were a kangaroo court where I was shouted at and ridiculed and was called a liar for not admitting to having learning difficulties/mental health issues. I tried to explain that Asperger's is not a mental health problem and I have an IQ of 137 so don't have learning difficulties but was shouted down. I attempted to take them to the Fair Employment Tribunal but had to drop it as I lacked the financial resources to employ lawyers. I am proud to have beaten 7600 others in a selection process designed by them and for them. It's like being one of the astronauts selected for the moon missions. The only thing that stopped me was illegal prejudice. I am now working in a factory."

This is the fear the keeps people from disclosing their AS and it is a valid concern:

> "ASDs often become targets of adverse disparate treatment and alienation. Occupations in law enforcement are not ready to accommodate ASDs. In my situation, I am armed and have a security clearance. I was thoroughly screened with many good character references. Yet, if I were to truly be myself at work, especially if I threw out the AS word, I would be rejected as being too defective to work as an armed officer."
>
> – SCOTT

What the employee can do:

- It is entirely up to you whether to disclose your AS or not.

- One belief is that if you are doing well in your job, and you tell others you have AS, then you are advancing the cause and reputation of people affected by ASDs.

- If you are having trouble in your working life, then disclosure might be a way to get some understanding and accommodation.

- Asking for what you need without full disclosure is another valid perspective. That may be enough for you.

- Others choose to "tough it out" and never ask for anything. But that doesn't mean we all can take that stance.

- Weigh your options carefully. Whatever you decide will impact your life.

- If and when you do disclose, do not do so "unarmed." Take your favorite short description of AS with you and give it to the person you are disclosing to, unless you are very good at describing it verbally. Others give a web address that contains a description they like. Urge whoever you are disclosing to, to read as much about Asperger's as they can and recommend some positive books or websites.

To employers and advocates:

If your employee hasn't told you that they have AS, you probably wouldn't be reading this book. You've taken the first steps to educate yourself about the condition. Even so, every individual with AS is different and they will all have differing abilities emotionally, intellectually, artistically, socially, etc. You cannot know what their limits are, so don't assume you do. Regardless of the law, it would be ethically questionable to fire someone for having AS. It would also be shutting the door on utilizing their numerous, sometimes amazing, gifts.

What are your thoughts on disclosure?

Have you had any positive or negative experiences from it?

How can you improve your chances for a positive result?

CHAPTER

"Bye Bye,"
Said the Black Sheep:
Avoiding the Asperger's
Pre-Emptive Strike

mployers should not lose a valuable employee over things that can be fixed. Nor should a person with AS leave a job they love for the wrong reason.

Some with AS will quit a job if they see termination or trouble on the horizon, just as some will quit school rather than fail. If an AS employee starts taking sick days or shows a decline in interest or performance, this could be the *Asperger's pre-emptive strike*. There is something—probably at work—that needs to be addressed to stop this happening.

> "I have rarely had big problems with bosses, because my work is usually good; however, I have quit jobs when I could see failure on the horizon. My problems have been with co-workers."
>
> – WALTER

> "The downfall came when I was pressured into jobs that made me communicate more with the 'team,' rising gas prices, and fear of layoff. I quit."
>
> – TOM

Sick days: Illness is a warning: It can be the result of environmental sensitivities, bullying, anxiety, etc. *Exhaustion* can occur from constant over-stimulation. *Depression and anxiety* are part of the autism package. As discussed earlier, there are many routes an individual can take to remedy that situation and most of us are very pro-active, acting as our own body detectives and trying various methods until we find our modus operandi. Suffice it to say that work problems can, in turn, cause more illness and stress, which can, in turn, cause more work problems, so this cycle needs to stop, preferably before it starts.

Stomach disorders are also common for those on the spectrum. Nine out of ten people interviewed for this book had gastrointestinal (GI) complaints, most commonly, IBS, ulcers, and even lesions on the intestines that had to be surgically removed. Most said their GI complaints were aggravated by stress.

Possible reasons for premature self-termination of employment:

- Social anxiety or fear of bullying
- Environment: too much sensory overload or unhealthy conditions
- Clothing, appearance, or similar restrictions—being expected to conform
- Lack of freedom in allocation of time and tasks
- Not being trusted. Being scrutinized.

- Being misunderstood, criticized, and doubted
- Not knowing whether or not their work is appreciated or up to standard
- Not having their strengths utilized. Asked or expected to do things that they are not good at
- A lack of job satisfaction. Not being stimulated or challenged.

> "I find it impossible to participate in a work life in any fully meaningful way. However, no one else seems to be bothered by the lack of meaning in things such as work. I've been told by a job coach that "work isn't there to challenge you" when I complained of never being able to really use my mind at work. My difficulty with work makes me feel so isolated sometimes I want to die. It's a big part of life, and I can't be a part of it in a way where I'm functioning as myself."
>
> – ALLISON

What the employee can do:

If the anxiety your job causes you has gotten to be too much and you are thinking about quitting, ask yourself if you've addressed all the issues in this book:

- **Have you asked for accommodation?**
- **Have you made your environment as comfortable and comforting as you could?**
- **Have you done your part to manage stress?** While many with AS say that things like yoga, meditation, and exercise have a positive but temporary effect on their anxiety, these things do have a cumulative effect and may lessen your reaction to, or increase your tolerance of, sensory triggers without you even realizing it. As stated, sensory issues have to be looked at as a total load. So does your general sense of well-being.

- **Did you try to find a mentor; someone to talk to?** Do you have a job advocate? A counselor? Is your boss someone who can be trusted?

- **Ask yourself if you like the *job*.** If you do, but it's the other aspects putting you off, re-read the previous chapters and make another effort to address these issues. If you are feeling unfulfilled or dissatisfied, take steps to do something about your education or skills. You may be able to elevate yourself without cutting loose from your current job.

- **Listen to your body and look to the source.** If you are experiencing physical illness or symptoms of stress, you can address them temporarily with medication, but look to the source. Investigate the benefits of fermented food, as discussed in *The Body Ecology Diet* by Donna Gates (2006), and *Gut and Psychology Syndrome* by Dr. Natasha Campbell-McBride (2004). Also popular among people who are trying to manage or improve ASD symptoms are the *GFCF* (gluten-free casein-free) diet and the *SCD* (specific carbohydrate diet). Even without going into such restrictive diets, one can *vastly* improve health and energy levels by eating healthily, i.e., staying away from processed foods, artificial ingredients, additives, etc.

- **Pull up your self-esteem.** Bullying and other problems at work can really get you down. Take a self-defense, martial arts, or other type of class to build your confidence. Celebrate your difference. Re-read or list all the positive traits of AS. Look at all the great things you've accomplished (probably on your own) and feel good about yourself. Money is a great confidence booster. There is no denying that. Find ways to increase your earnings or earning potential. Cutting loose from your current job (if that's what you're thinking of) without having a backup plan is not going to be good for your self-esteem.

- **Have other interests and activities to increase your enjoyment of life.** Your ability to hyper-focus and immerse yourself in a task means that you sometimes work too hard and get tunnel vision. Remind yourself to have fun; schedule social or pleasurable activities, things that make you happy and that take you out of yourself. Outside interests will increase self-confidence at work and may give you more things to talk about with others.

- **If you are unwilling to compromise or have tried but are unable to make things work,** self-employment may be your only viable option. Explore your options and follow your bliss, but be aware that you still need a fair number of the traits and people skills defined in this book to succeed, and that self-employment can mean lean times, at least for a while.

To employers and advocates:

Asperger's, health, stress management, and job satisfaction are all interrelated here and need to be looked at as a whole. If a good worker starts taking sick days, or seems to be detaching or retreating from the workplace, don't assume there's nothing you can do about it. Sit down with them and find out what has been going on. We have given you plenty of strategies to work with; these are all solutions within your grasp if you and your employee are willing.

Are you thinking about leaving your current position?

Do you have another job lined up or a plan of action?

Is there anything you can do to make your current situation better?

CHAPTER

REACH
to Succeed

I n the book *22 Things a Woman Must Know If She Loves a Man with Asperger's Syndrome* (2009), I stated that a relationship will stand a much better chance of succeeding if the person with AS will "REACH." The same applies to a professional relationship:

> **R**eceive a diagnosis, **E**ducate yourself about ASDs, **A**cknowledge the impact of Asperger's on your life, **C**ommit to the relationship, and seek **H**elp.

To put all the onus on your boss is unfair; personal beliefs and preferences aside, to expect the whole world to change around you is unrealistic. You have to accept that Asperger's Syndrome has given you gifts—in some cases, great gifts, but that there must have been some sort of trade-off, there must be some weaknesses within you. If you take a good, positive, but honest

look at yourself—your history, your patterns, you may begin to identify what those things might be.

It is your life, and you can make of it what you will. Don't let Asperger's defeat you when it can be your greatest ally.

To sum up:

- At least for the time being it seems that the autism spectrum population is growing.
- They are a significant number: 1% or more of the total population.
- There are significant differences in communication between spectrum and non-spectrum people. Some would say they are cultural differences.
- These differences need to be acknowledged and negotiated for economic reasons.
- In order to accomplish this, people with AS need training and support, as do employers.
- A person with AS has marketable and exceptional skills that are highly desirable in the workplace.
- A person with AS must manage his or her AS-related attributes to make long-term employment possible and pleasurable for themselves, their coworkers, and their employers. This would be made easier and more effective with the understanding and cooperation of the employer.

ADDITIONAL TOOLS

Finding the Perfect Job for YOU— The Personal Job Map

For people on the spectrum, choosing a job means taking into consideration more physical and social factors than it does for non-spectrum people. When planning your career, you must choose your path very carefully. One way to optimize success is to choose one that works with your strengths and interests and which doesn't involve too many of your shortcomings. While it may be a good idea to have some social contact, for example, to help you get used to people and develop some social skills, *too* much may just wear you down and make you feel bad about yourself. Temple Grandin stresses "social interaction through shared interests" which is another good reason to choose your job carefully. You'll be more comfortable being involved in a career with like-minded souls.

There are many *career aptitude* tests available, usually employing multiple choice questions, but people with Asperger's like being defined by ticking

boxes less than anyone, and those tests will probably not address the same concerns that someone on the spectrum might have. We can have a keen interest in a particular area, but have an equally keen aversion to aspects of the job. Just because a boy with Asperger's loves airplanes doesn't mean he wants to fly. Stephen Shore says in his article "Survival in the Workplace" (2008):

> I was miserable being involved in the business culture. The strange thing is, is that I find the *study* of business … fascinating. I also enjoy *teaching* business subjects … I just can't deal [with] *working* with the type of people who are in this field.

Most areas of career interest (if not all) can be studied, taught and/or practiced. As Stephen points out, one can be interested in one facet, but not the others. To identify your interests is a good start, but then you must define what application of those interests would make you the most happy and then break that down even further to include social, sensory, and other issues relevant to those with AS and HFA.

To this end, try making a **Personal Job Map** (see the chart at the end of this section).

- First, list your **Areas of Obsessive Interest**, whatever they are. They may be as disparate as horses, music, medicine, and engines. They can be specific or general. List anything that fascinates you, that you think you might like to have a career in.

- Next, there are columns for **Teaching, Practicing,** and **Studying.** Under each of these are BTA, *Triggers, and Solutions.*

  - BTA stands for *Best Things About.* Let's use *Music* as an example. Some BTAs of teaching music might include being immersed in a subject you are passionate about, teaching a whole new generation about the great music you love, and getting paid vacations to boot.

  - *Triggers* are strong aversions or whatever pushes your autistic buttons and over-stimulates you—things that you should avoid if possible. Still using music as our example, if sour notes, improperly played

instruments and stray mucous send you into stim-ville, teaching little kids might not be for you. Other triggers listed under "teaching" might be dealing with unruly behavior, standing up in front of a roomful of people, or getting up early and having to be somewhere every day at the same time. There are also bells and announcements as well as smells and germs and halls teeming with people. In every job or career, there might be a million triggers lurking, waiting to trip you up and ruin your day. You must identify what those might be and decide if and how you are going to handle them. You must decide if the sensory issues that will confront you are things you are willing to try to overcome. Let us not forget that we can work on our overall health and happiness and take steps to desensitize ourselves to certain triggers. There comes a point for everyone on the spectrum where earning money means facing our fears and winning.

– *Solutions* are usually there if you look for them, and they will consist of working with what you want to work with while avoiding as many of your triggers as possible. Solutions to the above might be: teaching at college level, or teaching one-on-one, part-time, for example, at a music store or in people's homes.

• *Practicing* in this case, means playing music for a living. Major triggers under this heading might be the socializing one might have to do, and unpredictable hotel rooms if one is touring. Lack of a steady paycheck is not necessarily a trigger but it is a 'con' and should be listed, since financial stability keeps stress levels down. A possible *solution* to these things might be working as a house musician for a studio or club, or playing with an orchestra if one is skilled enough.

• Under *Studying* you can list what relevant qualifications you already possess and what, if anything, you need to acquire as well as where you can go to get it—i.e., what university, college, or technical school.

At the end of this section is a sample of what the table could look like. Make copies of this table as you may want to fill it out more than once. Before you do so, you may find it helpful to create a master list of Areas of Obsessive Interest on a separate sheet, as well as a complete list of triggers

to really acquaint yourself with what you love and what you don't, what turns you on and what ticks you off. Once you fill out the Job Map, your strongest triggers—things you absolutely want to avoid—need to be crossed out, or colored in red. Your strongest BTAs—things you absolutely require or desire should be bolded, circled, or colored in a favorite color. So should your best solutions.

When you are finished, have a look at what your worst triggers are, and then focus on your brightest, boldest BTAs. In the **Course of Action or Realization** box, write down your impressions based on your answers. The responses should help you form a plan or give you some important things to think about. You might find that by combining elements of different passions, you discover an area you could work in that you hadn't considered before. You might find you are currently in the wrong field, but that you have identified what it is that you would like to do. You might even discover that you *are* in the right field, but the wrong application. You might ascertain that a degree is necessary to get you where you want to go. You might even discover that you are in the right field or job already, and that by applying some of the suggestions in this book, you'll have what you need for career fulfillment.

While some of our Areas of Obsessive Interest are not immediately marketable, or may not be obviously linked to our proper vocation, I believe that they contain the seeds, the clues, to our perfect career. We need to be excited about our job in order to put our Asperger attributes to good use. By cross-referencing in this way, by the time you get done with this exercise, you should have some sort of viable "map" to choosing your career. You should have a vision for your immediate and long-term future. And remember, these are your own words and thoughts, not someone else's advice for you.

PERSONAL JOB MAP

Area of Obsessive Interest	TEACHING			PRACTICING			STUDYING		
	BTA	Triggers	Solutions	BTA	Triggers	Solutions	What I Have	What I Need	Where/How
		• • •			• • •				
		• • •			• • •				
		• • •			• • •				

Course of Action/Realization:

Interview Tips for Those With Asperger's

1. Dress appropriately for the type of position you are seeking. There are big differences between retail, factory, office, coffeehouse, or outdoor positions. Use magazines, TV shows, job coaches, friends, family, or salespeople to get some advice on what to wear.

2. Make sure your clothing is clean and doesn't have stains or tears. Don't wear it inside out! (That *had* to be said.)

3. Hair, beard, and nails should be groomed appropriate to the position.

4. Don't overdo cologne (you probably don't wear it anyway) and make sure you have no body odor.

5. If eye contact is difficult for you, practice making brief eye contact with someone close to you and not flinching. Don't overdo it and stare. At the interview have two copies of your resume so you both have something to look at besides each other.

A portfolio is even better, because you can look at it together, and for longer periods of time.

6. A resume will also help you keep your facts straight, in case you get confused.

7. When you are answering questions and talking about yourself, don't talk for more than a couple of minutes at a time. Think of conversation as reciprocal, like a relaxed game of tennis.

8. If asked about your interests, be careful not to give away too much or for too long. (They probably won't understand your anime obsession at an insurance firm.)

9. If you do not disclose AS at the interview, do not feel guilty or sneaky. We all have health issues (the boss probably does too), and we shouldn't thrust them forward when trying to make a good first impression.

10. Don't speak ill of past bosses, co-workers, or companies, or talk about how you were abused, etc. It will be awkward for the employer and make you look like a whiner as opposed to a winner.

11. Stay positive. It takes conscious effort.

12. Don't slouch in your chair. Make sure your shoulders are down and relaxed. Things mentioned earlier like yoga, martial arts, sports, dance, etc., will help you become more conscious of your body language.

13. If you sense during the interview that you won't like the job, don't take it just to prove you can. You'll only be wasting everyone's time, including your own. Have standards and stick to them.

14. If you don't get the first job you try for, don't give up. It probably wasn't right for you. Keep trying until you get what you need!

Notes

Use these pages to list your own tips, reminders, and ideas.

_____

_____

_____

_____

_____

_____

_____

_____

_____

_____

References

American Psychiatric Association. (2000). *Diagnostic and Statistical Manual of Mental Disorders DSM-IV-TR Fourth Edition, Text Revision.* Washington, DC: American Psychiatric Association.

Campbell-McBride, N. (2004). *Gut and Psychology Syndrome: Natural Treatment for Autism, ADD/ADHD, Dyslexia, Dyspraxia, Depression, Schizophrenia.* Cambridge: Medinform Publishing.

Carter, P., Russell, K. (2001). *Psychometric Testing1000 ways to Assess Your Personality, Creativity and Lateral Thinking.* Chichester: J. Wiley and Sons.

Caruso St. John Architects. *Origins of the Office: History of the Office.* Accessed on February 2, 2009 at www.carusostjohn.com/artscouncil/ history/taylorist/index.html.

CDC (Center for Disease Control). *Autism: Frequently Asked Questions,* para.5, *What do the ADDM network results tell us about the prevalence of ASD in the United States?* Accessed on February 18, 2009 at www.cdc.gov/ncbddd/autism/faq_prevalence.htm#whatisprevalence.

De Vries, J. (2007). *Perfectionism in Asperger's* Accessed on February 15, 2009 at www.asperger-advice.com/asperger-perfectionism.html.

Edwards, L., Torcellini, P. (2002). *A Literature Review of the Effects of Natural Light on Building Occupants.* Colorado: U.S. Department of Energy.

Employment Act 2002. Accessed on February 26, 2009 at www.opsi.gov.uk/about/copyright-notice.htm Crown copyright 2002 - 2008.

Factor, P. (2006). *Two Stops Short of Dagenham.* Accessed on February 2, 2009 at www.simple-talk.com/opinion/opinion-pieces/two-stops-short-of-dagenham.

Farrell, E. (2004). Asperger's Confounds Colleges: A surge of students diagnosed with an autism-related disorder poses new challenges. *The Chronicle of Higher Education, 51,* 7, A35.

Fawcett, T. (2004). *Working From Home Trend Gathers Pace* Accessed on February 26, 2009 at http://news.bbc.co.uk/1/hi/business/3645475.stm BBC News.

Fitzgerald, M. (2005). "Asperger's Syndrome and Adult Outcomes." Asperger's Syndrome Conference (Autism Cymru). Millennium Stadium, Cardiff.

Gates, D. (2006). *The Body Ecology Diet 10th.* Georgia: Body Ecology.

Grandin, T. (1995, 2006). *Thinking in Pictures.* New York: Vintage.

Hayashi, M., Kato, M., Igarashi, K., Kashima, H. (2008). "Superior fluid intelligence in children with Asperger's disorder." *Brain and Cognition, 66,* 3, 306-310.

Hendrickx, S. (2009). *Asperger Syndrome and Employment: What People with Asperger Syndrome Really Really Want.* London: Jessica Kingsley Publishers.

Hesman Saey, T. (2008). "Asperger's Syndrome May Not Lead to Lack of Empathy". Accessed on March 9, 2009 at www.sciencenews.org/view/generic/id/31400/title/Asperger%E2%80%99s_syndrome_may_not_lead_to_lack_of_empathy_.

Human Resource Village. *The Work Environment and Employee Productivity.* Accessed on March 27, 2009 at www.hrvillage.com/human-resources/employee-productivity.htm.

Keashly, L. & Jagatic, K. (2003). *Bullying and Emotional Abuse in the Workplace.* Stale, Einarsen et al. London: Taylor and Francis.

Kelly, E. & Kalev, A. (2006). "Managing flexible work arrangements in US organizations: formalized discretion or 'a right to ask." *Socio-Economic Review 4,* 3, 379-416.

Mahari, A. (2009). *You Don't Seem Like You Have Asperger's.* Accessed January 15, 2009 at http://aspergeradults.ca.

Medical Research Council. (2007). *Tuning Out: Researchers Make Sense of Background Noise.* London: Medical Research Council.

Müller, E., Schuler, A., Burton, B. & Yates G. *Vocational Supports For Individuals With Asperger Syndrome.* Accessed on April 1, 2009 at www.autistics.org/JVRpaper.htm.

Myles, B., Trautman, M. & Schelvan, R. (2004). *The Hidden Curriculum.* Kansas: Autism Asperger Publishing Company.

Namie, G., Namie, R. (2003). *The Bully at Work, Rev Ed.* Washington: The Bullying Institute.

National Autistic Society, The. (2005). *Employing People with Asperger Syndrome: A Practical Guide.* London: The National Autistic Society.

National Autistic Society, The. (2009). *High-Functioning Autism and Asperger Syndrome: What's the Difference?* London: The National Autistic Society. Accessed on February 11, 2009 at www.nas.org.uk/nas/jsp/polopoly.jsp?d=1049&a=3337.

Nelson, D. (2009). "Director's Commentary: Control." *TCS Newsletter* Georgia: The Community School.

Nichols, B. *What is Asperger's?* Accessed on March 1, 2009 at http://Asperger's-tucson.org/what_is_Asperger's.

Oldham, G., Brass, D. (1979). "Employee Reactions to an Open-Plan Office: A Naturally Occurring Quasi-Experiment." *Administrative Science Quarterly*, 24, 2, 267-284.

Oommen, V., Knowles, M., Zhao, I. (2008). Should Health Service Managers Embrace Open Plan Work Environments? A Review *Asia Pacific Journal of Health Management* 3, 2, 37.

Pounds, J. (2008). *Positive Reinforcement – It's a Relationship.* Accessed on March 27, 2009 at http://the-positive-manager.blogspot.com/2008/02/leading-with-reinforcing-relationships.html.

Rowe, J. *Psychometric Tests.* Accessed on March 27, 2009 at www.primecareers.co.uk/prca/PCContent.nsf/idflat/5NLJE2MHER!opendocument.

Schwarz, J. (2002). "New book is road map to help parents 'find' their child who has Asperger syndrome or high-functioning autism" University of Washington News. Accessed on February 15, 2009 at http://uwnews.org/article.asp?articleID=2430.

Shore, S. *Survival in the Workplace.* Accessed on October 19, 2008 at http://www.udel.edu/bkirby/asperger/survival_shore.html#Survival.

Simone, R. (2009). *22 Things a Woman Must Know If She Loves a Man with Asperger's Syndrome.* London: Jessica Kingsley Publishers.

United States Environmental Protection Agency. (1991). *Indoor Air Facts No. 4 (revised) Sick Building Syndrome.* Washington DC: EPA.

Wikipedia. (2008). *Alexythimia,* Accessed on March 3, 2009 at http://en.wikipedia.org/wiki/Alexithymia.

Wikipedia. (2008). *Fluid and crystallized intelligence.* Accessed on March 3, 2009 at http://en.wikipedia.org/wiki/Fluid_and_crystallized_intelligence.

WBI - Zogby International. (2007). "As Labor Day Nears, Workplace Bullying Institute Survey Finds Half of Working Americans Affected by Workplace Bullying." New York: Zogby International. Accessed on 4/1/09 at www.zogby.com/news/readnews.cfm?ID=1353.

Yamada, D. (2007). Potential Legal protections and Liabilities for Workplace Bullying. Massachusetts: New Workplace Institute.

Young, R. (1999). "A sound business plan (Designing better acoustics for today's open offices)." *Building Design & Construction, 40*, 6, 84.

Resources

Educational Programs

The Community School

www.thecommunityschool.net
303 Claremont Ave. Decatur, Georgia. 30030
404.308.8548
FOUNDER: Dave Nelson

"The Community School is designed for students in junior high and high school (ages 12-18 years old) who have had difficulty keeping pace in traditional academic settings, and who need more emphasis on social-emotional development, communication and relationship skills, and contextual, experiential learning. This program offers a nurturing and highly interactive learning environment built around experiences of strong personal interest. We are accredited by the Georgia Accrediting Commission, enabling students who are ready to work towards a high school diploma to do so."

The program is limited. For more information visit *www.thecommunityschool.net*

ASAT: The Asperger Syndrome Adult Transition program
(at South Connecticut State University)
www.chapelhavenaspergerprogram.org
203.397.1714
DIRECTOR: Judy Lefkowitz

Chapel Haven, a private nonprofit agency founded in 1971, is dedicated to helping adults with special challenges live independent and productive lives, and is proud to offer an Asperger's Syndrome Adult Transition Program. ASAT is designed to address the needs of this currently underserved population.

Contact information/admissions applications available at their website.

Pathway at UCLA Extension
www.uclaextension.edu/pathway
Pathway—UCLA Extension
10995 Le Conte Avenue, Suite 413
Los Angeles, CA 90024
310.794.1235
pathway@uclaextension.edu

Pathway is a two-year certificate program for students with developmental disabilities, providing a blend of educational, social, and vocational experiences, taught and supervised by an expertly trained staff that is sensitive to the individual needs of our students.

On campus, students attend intimate-sized classes and participate in the many social, recreational, and cultural activities of a major university. They engage with other students and enjoy learning opportunities for career exploration through coursework and employment on and near the UCLA campus.

Other Websites

www.autismhangout.com
News, videos, webinars and programs all about autism and Asperger Syndrome. A marvelous resource passionately run by Craig Evans.

www.grasp.org
GRASP—The Global and Regional Asperger Syndrome Partnership
666 Broadway, Suite 830
New York, NY 10012
1.888.474.7277 (888.47.GRASP) phone and fax
EXECUTIVE DIRECTOR: Michael John Carley,
info@grasp.org

www.help4Asperger's.com
Rudy Simone's official web site.

www.templegrandin.com
The website of a true pioneer, animal scientist, and author. You must read one of her books and see her speak if you really want to understand the wondrous nature of Asperger's and autism.

www.workplacebullying.org
The Bullying Institute. The website of Drs. Gary and Ruth Namie: *"Because Work Shouldn't Hurt."*

Books

Myles, B., Trautman, M., & Schelvan, R. (2004). *The Hidden Curriculum.* Kansas: Autism Asperger Publishing Company.

Hendrickx, S. (2009). *Asperger Syndrome and Employment: What People with Asperger Syndrome Really Really Want.* London: Jessica Kingsley Publishers.

Meyer R. (2001). *Asperger Syndrome Employment Workbook.* London: Jessica Kingsley Publishers.

Films

Laura Ziskin (Producer) & James L. Brooks (Director). (1997) *As Good As it Gets* [Motion picture]. United States: TriStar pictures

Jack Nicholson's obsessive-compulsive character has many classic Aspergian traits. The whole film is about relinquishing control and allowing in the unpredictable, mainly in the form of people and relationships.

Lawrence, R. (Producer) & Næss, P. (Director). (2005). *Mozart and the Whale* [Motion picture]. United States: Big City Pictures. Based on the book by Newport, J., Newport M., and Dodd, J.

The book/movie is a true story of the relationship between two people with Asperger's Syndrome.

Max Mayer, (Director). (2009). *Adam* [Motion picture]. United States: Fox Searchlight Pictures.

The story of a man with Asperger's and his relationship/employment challenges and triumphs.

Government Agencies

U.S. Department of Justice
Americans with Disabilities Act
www.ada.gov

U.S. Equal Employment Opportunity Commission
131 M Street, NE
Washington, DC 20507
Phone: 202.663.4900
TTY: 202.663.4494
1.800.669.4000
info@eeoc.gov

Software

http://chatterblocker.com
(software programs that block out noise)

Support Groups

Southern Arizona Association of Adult Asperger's
Tucson, AZ
http://Asperger's-tucson.org/homepage
520.954.1490
FOUNDER: Dr. Barbara Nichols

A support network for adults with Asperger's and their family members.

Index